YOUR LIFE 4

JOHN FOSTER
KIM RICHARDSON
SIMON FOSTER

Collins

William Collins' dream of knowledge for all began with the publication of his first book in 1819. A self-educated mill worker, he not only enriched millions of lives, but also founded a flourishing publishing house. Today, staying true to this spirit, Collins books are packed with inspiration, innovation and a practical expertise. They place you at the centre of a world of possibility and give you exactly what you need to explore it.

Collins. Do more.

Published by Collins
An imprint of HarperCollinsPublishers
77–85 Fulham Palace Road
Hammersmith
London
W6 8JB

Browse the complete Collins catalogue at
www.collinseducation.com

10 9 8 7 6 5 4 3 2 1

ISBN 0 00 719406 4

John Foster, Simon Foster and Kim Richardson assert their moral right to be identified as the authors of this work

British Library Cataloguing in Publication Data. A Catalogue record for this publication is available from the British Library

Commissioned by Thomas Allain-Chapman
Managed by Abigail Woodman
Project managed by Nancy Candlin
Edited by Alyson Jones
Cover and internal design by bluepig design
Page make-up by JPD
Cover photograph: Pixland 2002/Bruno Coste
Text permissions by Jackie Newman
Photographic permissions by Thelma Gilbert
Production by Katie Butler
Printed and bound by Imago
Consultant reader: Jackie Reynolds, Mill Hill County High School, London

Acknowledgements

The Publishers gratefully acknowledge the following for permission to reproduce copyright material. Whilst every effort has been made to trace the copyright holders, in cases where this has been unsuccessful or if any have inadvertently been overlooked, the Publishers will be pleased to make the necessary arrangements at the first opportunity.

TEXT EXTRACTS: 'Teenagers "too idle" to bother with good food' by Rober Uhlig, Daily Telegraph, 14th October 2003. © Telegraph Group Limited, 2003. Reprinted with permission; 'Junk food adverts to be banned in crackdown on obesity' by Rachel Dobson and Paul Marinko, The Sunday Times, 9th November 2003. © NI Syndication, London, 2003. Reprinted with permission; 'Put VAT on high-fat food, urges GP by David Derbyshire', Daily Telegraph, 10th June, 2003. © Telegraph Group Limited, 2003. Reprinted with permission; 'Linekar denies fuelling obesity by Sarah Womack', Daily Telegraph, 14th November, 2003. © Telegraph Group Limited, 2003. Reprinted with permission; 'Junk food chiefs dish out the blame for obesity by Robert Uhlig', Daily Telegraph, 28th November, 2003. © Telegraph Group Limited, 2003. Reprinted with permission; 'What you think about your bodies' and 'Develop healthy eating habits' is adapted from an article in BLISS February 2004. Reprinted with permission of EMAP Elan Syndications; Extracts from But You Don't Understand Me by Elaine Sishton and Charlotte Russell, published by John Hunt Publishing Limited. Reprinted with permission; Extracts from 'To do it or not to do it' from Cosmo Girl! magazine 7/03 p 78. Courtesy of Cosmo Girl! Magazine © National Magazine Company. Reprinted with permission; Extract from Sex Ed by Dr. Miriam Stoppard, published by Dorling Kindersley, © 1997 Dorling Kindersley, text copyright © 1997 by Miriam Stoppard. Reprinted by permission of Penguin Group UK; 'The low down on contraception' and 'The low down on pregnancy' taken from an article in J17 February 2004 'Let's Talk About Sex'. Reprinted by permission of Emap Elan Syndications; Extracts taken from 'Thrills, Pills and Contraception' US Cosmo Girl! September 2003 pp 80–81; 'Clubbers warned to wear earplugs or risk deafness' by David Brindle, The Guardian, 3rd August, 1999. © Guardian Newspapers Limited 1999. Reprinted with permission; 'Doctors vote to ban TV adverts "gloryfying" drink

by Celia Hall', Daily Telegraph, 3rd July, 2003. © Telegraph Group Limited, 2003. Reprinted with permission; 'Doctors call for health warnings on alcohol' by Celia Hall, Daily Telegraph, 24th July, 2003. © Telegraph Group Limited, 2003. Reprinted with permission; Extracts from XY – A Toolkit For Life by Matt Whyman, published by Hodder. Reprinted with permission of Hodder & Stoughton Limited; 'Ban smoking in public, says senior doctors' by Celia Hall, Daily Telegraph, 26th November, 2003. © Telegraph Group Limited, 2003. Reprinted with permission; 'Screen smokers need X-rating to protect teenagers' by David Derbyshire, Daily Telegraph, 10th June, 2003. © Telegraph Group Limited, 2003. Reprinted with permission; Extract from Talking Dirty by Elaine Sishton and Charlotte Russell, published by John Hunt Publishing. Reprinted with permission; Extract from 'Body piercing is rite of passage as well as fashion' by Jeremy Lawrence, The Independent, 8 March 2003 © Independent Newspapers 2003. Reprinted with permission; 'Young are still dying for a suntan' by Sam Lister, The Times, 31 March, 2004. © NI Syndication, 2004. Reprinted with permission; Extracts from 'How "binge" sunbathers risk their lives for a tan' by Jenny Hope, in The Daily Mail, 25 April, 2001. Reprinted with permission; 'Spotlight on acne', first published in Health Wise Winter 1997 by Dr Daron Seukeran Copyright © Dr. Daron Seukeran. Reprinted with the kind permission of the author; 'It happens to us all' extracts taken from 'The Issue: Bereavement' TES 3/9/02. Pp 16–17. Reprinted with permission of TES; 'Culture Club' by Dinah Starkey, from 'RESPECT', TES SUPPLEMENT 4 JULY 2003 pg 6. Copyright © Dinah Starkey 2003. Reprinted with the kind permission of the author; 'Susan takes good care of us' from Inner Voice Birmingham City Council, February 2004 pg 7. Reprinted with permission; 'Britain's benefit' from www.cre.gov.uk. Reprinted with permission of CRE; 'Tebbit's cricket loyalty test hit for six' by John Carvel, Social Affairs editor, in The Guardian, 8th January, 2004. © Guardian Newspapers Limited, 2004. Reprinted with permission; 'Roots and Branches' by Nadia Marks, from The Guardian, 17th March, 2004. © Nadia Marks 2004 Reprinted with permission; Extract from 'Is It Legal?' leaflet produced by NFPI (National Family & Parenting Institute). Reprinted with permission; Extracts taken from www.tradingstandards.gov.uk reprinted with permission; Quote by Caroline Hamilton reprinted with permission; Quote by Lyn Costello; Extracts from 'A day in the life of yob-culture Britain' by Philip Johnston, The Telegraph, 15th October, 2003. © Telegraph Newspapers 2003. Reprinted with permission; 'Using new tools to attack the roots of crime' by Nick Davies, The Guardian, July 12th, 2003. © Nick Davies 2003. Reprinted with the kind permission of the author; Extracts from 'Running a mock trial' found at www.citizenshipfoundation.org.uk. Reprinted with permission; Extracts from 'Barring the Way to Success' by Lucie Russell, from The Big Issue, April 28–May 4 2003. Reprinted with permission; Extracts from 'Beckham trounces Jesus in poll to find youth heroes' The Daily Mail 26 January, 2004. Reprinted with permission; Extracts from 'Life: this week: Why do women care less about looks than men?' by Ian Sample, The Guardian, 22nd April, 2004. © Guardian Newspapers Limited 2004. Reprinted with permission; Extract about designer clothes by Wayne Hemmingway. Reprinted with the kind permission of the author; Extract from 'The Gay Rapper: He's white, he's English, he's homosexual. Can Qboy possibly fit into the notoriously bigoted world of hip hop?' by Hattie Collins, The Guardian 16th April 2004. © Guardian Newspapers Limited 2004. Used with permission; Extracts slightly adapted from Sisters Unlimited by Jessica Howie, published by Vermilion. Used by permission of The Random House Group Limited; Extracts from www.raisingkids.co.uk. Reprinted with their kind permission; Extracts from Being a Happy Teenager by Andrew Matthews. Copyright © Andrew Matthews. Reprinted with the kind permission of Seashell Publishers Pty Ltd, Australia; Quotes by Mary Bousted reprinted with permission; 'Celebrities now more influential than parents' by Sarah Cassidy, The Independent 1 March 2004. © Independent Newspapers 2004. Reprinted with permission; 'How to be assertive without being aggressive' by Caro Handley; Extracts from 'A quarrel a day…' from 19 magazine, March 2004 pg 28 © IPC Syndication/19. Some extracts in this article are taken from Make Love Work For You by Anne Nicholls, Piatkus. Extracts reprinted with permission of IPC Syndication and Piatkus; 'Why girls should argue with mother' by Alison Chiesa, Herald, 14 April 2004. Reprinted with permission of Newsquest (Herald and Times) Limited; Extracts belonging to Prospects reprinted with permission; Extract from Keep Your Options Open by Vivienne Neale, published by Hodder. Reprinted with permission of Hodder & Stoughton Limited; Extract from Connexions Step Two Booklet and Options at 16 Crown Copyright ©; Extract from Issues 4 edited by John Foster, published by Collins Educational © HarperCollinsPublishers 1992; Two extracts from Chalkface.com Reprinted with permission; 'School leavers can't budget, says research' by Rebecca Smithers, The Guardian, April 29th 2002. © The Guardian. Reprinted with permission; 'Why do I need a bank account' from www.fsa.go.uk; Extract from Young Citizen's Passport, by Tony Thorpe, published by Hodder & Stoughton Educational. © 2003 by the Citizenship Foundation. Reprinted with permission of Hodder Arnold; Extract from Adolescence: The Survival Guide for Parents and Teenagers by E Fenwick and T Smith (Dorling Kindersley Revised Edition 1998) Copyright © Dorling Kindersley 1998. Reprinted with permission of Penguin Group UK; Extracts from Girls' Talk by Maria Pallotta-Chiarolli, published by Finch Publishing Pty Ltd, Australia pp 61–3 1998. Reprinted with the kind permission of the author; Extract from Boys About Boys by Nick Fisher, published by Pan Macmillan 1991. Reprinted with permission of the publishers; Extract from Tell It Like It Is by Katie Masters published by Virgin Books. Copyright © Katie Masters, 2002 Virgin Books Limited. Reprinted by permission of Virgin Books Ltd; 'Degrees of separation' by John James, The Guardian, 24th July, 2002. © The Guardian. Reprinted with permission; Extract from 'Children: Real Victims of Divorce', The Times, February 19th, 2004. © NI Syndication 2004. Reprinted with permission; Extracts from www.childbereavement.org.uk. Reprinted with permission; Extract taken from rd4u.org.uk reprinted with permission of Cruse Bereavement Care; Extracts from www.electoral-reform.org.uk Reprinted with permission; 'I feel ashamed says Sophie 16' taken from an article in J17 February 2004 entitled 'Just Say No!'. Reprinted by permission of Emap Elan Syndications

PHOTOS: Collections/Roger Scruton p6; Corbis p8; Corbis p10; Rex Features p12; Topham Picturepoint p13; Bubbles p14; Photofusion p16tl, S & R Greenhills p16tr, Photofusion p16bl & br; Getty p17; Rex Features p19; Topham Picturepoint p21; Rex Features p23; Topham Picturepoint p24; BBC p26t, Photofusion p26b; Photofusion p27; Photofusion p29; Rex Features p30; Topham Picturepoint p35; Rex Features p38; UK Youth Parliament p39; Photofusion p42; Rex Features p45; Bubbles p46; Greg Frederick p48; Alamy p49; Alamy p50; Rex Features p51; Getty p53; Topham Picturepoint p57; Bubbles p58; Roger Scruton p63; Rex Features p66; S & R Greenhills p69; SPL p71; Rex Features p73; Rex Features p75; S & R Greenhills p77; Rex Features p79; Bubbles p81; Bubbles p82; S & R Greenhills p83; Getty p85; Rex Features p86; Bubbles p89; Bubbles p90t, Rex Features p90b; Bubbles p91; Topham Picturepoint p93

CONTENTS

INTRODUCTION

Your Life at Key Stage 4 (14–16)

Your Life 4 and Your Life 5 together form a comprehensive two-year course in Personal, Social and Health Education, and Citizenship at Key Stage 4. This table shows how the eleven PSHE units and eight Citizenship units cover the requirements of the National Framework for PSHE and the National Curriculum Programme of Study for Citizenship.

CITIZENSHIP
Developing as a citizen

These units aim to help you to understand how you can play a full part as a citizen in British society.

YEAR 4

- **UNIT 1** Britain – a diverse society (Citizenship 1b, 2a, 2b, 2c)
- **UNIT 2** Human rights (Citizenship 1a, 2a, 2b, 2c)
- **UNIT 3** Rights and responsibilities (Citizenship 1a, 1h, 2a, 2b, 2c)
- **UNIT 4** The law of the land (Citizenship 1a, 1c, 2a, 2b, 2c)
- **UNIT 5** Crime and punishment (Citizenship 1a, 2a, 2b, 2c)
- **UNIT 6** It's your government (Citizenship 1c, 1d, 2a, 2b, 2c)
- **UNIT 7** It's your council (Citizenship 1d, 1f, 2a, 2b, 2c, 3b)
- **UNIT 8** Working for change (Citizenship 1f, 2a, 2b, 2c, 3b, 3c)

YEAR 5

- **UNIT 1** The UK and its relations with the rest of the world (Citizenship 1i, 2a, 2b, 2c)
- **UNIT 2** Human rights (Citizenship 1a, 2a, 2b, 2c)
- **UNIT 3** Media matters (Citizenship 1g, 2a, 2b, 2c)
- **UNIT 4** How the economy works (Citizenship 1e, 2a, 2b, 2c)
- **UNIT 5** The global economy (Citizenship 1e, 2a, 2b, 2c)
- **UNIT 6** Global challenges (Citizenship 1j, 2a, 2b, 2c)
- **UNIT 7** Environmental issues (Citizenship 1j, 2a, 2b, 2c)
- **UNIT 8** Working for change (Citizenship 1f, 2a, 2b, 2c, 3b, 3c)

The activities

The various activities offer you the opportunity to develop a number of important skills:

- To analyse information and to research further information from a range of sources, including the internet (Citizenship 2a)

- To share your views on more topical political, social and moral issues in class discussions and debates, justifying your opinions (Citizenship 2b, 2c)

- To express your ideas in a variety of written forms (Citizenship 2b)

- To reflect on your personal qualities, and to assess your character, achievements and potential so that you can set yourself realistic personal goals (PSHE 1a)

- To understand your emotions and how to manage them in your relationships with family and friends (PSHE 3e)

- To know how to make informed choices and how to make your own decisions (PSHE 1d)

- To take responsibility for your own health, welfare and safety (PSHE 2a)

- To recognise when unhelpful pressure is being put on you, and to use assertive techniques to combat it (PSHE 2b)

PERSONAL, SOCIAL AND HEALTH EDUCATION

Understanding yourself

This strand of the course aims to develop your confidence and responsibility.

Keeping healthy

These units are designed to help you to understand how to develop a healthy, safer lifestyle, to think about the alternatives when making decision about personal health, and the consequences of such decisions.

Developing relationships

The aim of these units is to develop your ability to handle close relationships and to emphasise the importance of showing respect and acting responsibly in your dealings with other people.

Reviewing

This unit provides a framework for assessing the knowledge, skills and understanding developed in Citizenship, and Personal, Social and Health Education during the year.

UNIT 9 Developing your identity (PSHE 1a, 1b, 1c, 1d)	**UNIT 13** Healthy eating (PSHE 2a, 2d)	**UNIT 17** Changing relationships: friends and family (PSHE 3b, 3e, 3f 3h)	**UNIT 20** Reviewing and recording (PSHE 1a/Citizenship 3c)
UNIT 10 Managing your emotions and moods (PSHE 1a, 1b, 1c, 1d, 3e, 3f)	**UNIT 14** Safer sex and contraception (PSHE 2a, 2b, 2e, 2f, 3b)	**UNIT 18** Coping with crises (PSHE 3e, 3f, 3i, 3j)	
UNIT 11 Thinking ahead: planning your future (PSHE 1f, 1g)	**UNIT 15** Drinking and smoking (PSHE 2a, 2b, 2e)	**UNIT 19** Challenging offensive behaviour (PSHE 3a, 3c/Citizenship 1b, 2a, 2b, 2c)	
UNIT 12 Managing your money (PSHE 1e)	**UNIT 16** Health matters (PSHE 2a, 2e, 2g)		
UNIT 9 Developing your own values (PSHE 1b/Citizenship 2a, 2b, 2c)	**UNIT 13** Managing stress and dealing with depression (PSHE 2c)	**UNIT 17** Marriage and commitment (PSHE 3e, 3g)	**UNIT 21** Reviewing and recording (PSHE 1a/Citizenship 3c)
UNIT 10 Managing your time and studies (PSHE 1a)	**UNIT 14** Safer sex (PSHE 2a, 2b, 2e, 2f, 3b)	**UNIT 18** Parenthood and parenting (PSHE 3h)	
UNIT 11 Thinking ahead: planning your future (PSHE 1f, 1g)	**UNIT 15** Drugs and drugtaking (PSHE 2a, 2b, 2e)	**UNIT 19** Challenging offensive behaviour (PSHE 3a, 3c/Citizenship 1a, 2a, 2b, 2c)	
UNIT 12 Managing your money (PSHE 1e)	**UNIT 16** Emergency First Aid (PSHE 2h)	**UNIT 20** Co-operating on a community project (Citizenship 1f, 2a, 2b, 2c, 3b, 3c)	

1 BRITAIN – A DIVERSE SOCIETY

How did Britain begin?

Aim: To explore the origins of Britain as a multicultural and multiethnic society, and the benefits that this has brought (Citizenship 1b, 2a, 2b, 2c)

Culture club

The English nation has been made by migration – and is all the better for it, says Dinah Starkey

The English are the product of centuries of migration, some peaceful, some forcible. John Bull, the typical Englishman, may in fact be two parts Germanic Saxon to one part Celt, with a chunk of Scandinavian, a smattering of French and a dash of West Indian, Asian, Jewish or Irish. The asylum seekers who enter our country today are only the latest immigrants.

Scotland and Wales have had their newcomers too, but England has always been a bigger melting pot. The Scots and the Welsh kept their native languages and culture for much longer, and even now they have a separate identity.

Go back 40,000 years and the original ancient Britons were arriving from continental Europe. They were followed, much later, by the Beaker people, who brought with them skills in working the mysterious new metal – bronze.

The Celts arrived about 700BC, and with them came the Iron Age. Next were the Romans in 43AD. They stayed for nearly 400 years, transforming the landscape with road systems, farming methods and new crops. Many of the towns they established still survive.

By 410AD the Roman empire was crumbling and the Angles and Saxons began to raid across the sea from what is now Germany. It was the Saxons who named the shires and villages, and the English language began to take shape.

The Normans, themselves the descendants of the Vikings, held all things Saxon in contempt and invaded in 1066. They ignored the native language and continued to speak Norman French for generations. But the locals went on using Saxon and gradually the two languages began to merge.

As trade routes opened in Tudor times, African boys were brought to Britain to satisfy the fashionable demand for black servants, called blackamoors. By the end of Queen Elizabeth I's reign in 1603, an estimated 20,000 'blackamoors' were living and working in London.

The Huguenots, a French Protestant group, flooded into Britain in the 17th century to escape persecution by Catholic France. Many were cloth workers and they brought with them techniques which revitalised the British textile industry. In the 19th century, tens of thousands of Irish immigrants came to England after the potato famine, and from 1881 mounting persecution in Eastern Europe and Russia led to the arrival of thousands of Jews.

The evolution of the British national identity has been slow and painful. The struggle for success that has faced each generation of immigrants continues today. Perhaps we can help to make the process of assimilation a little easier by teaching children about their past. That way they may come to understand what incomers have brought to our country and what they might contribute in the centuries to come.

FROM AN ARTICLE BY DINAH STARKEY IN THE *TES SUPPLEMENT* 'RESPECT

Britain's benefit

Britain has benefited from ethnic diversity throughout its history. From industry and commerce to art and dance, from sport and music to science and literature, the activities of individuals and groups from ethnic minorities have enriched life in Britain for all.

Newcomers have often met hostility and resentment, yet even a quick study would show that they have brought skills and qualifications, set up businesses and created jobs, not only for themselves but also for local people. Many have been willing to do jobs that have been difficult to fill locally. What is remarkable and often not understood is that the contributions immigrants and their immediate descendants have made – and continue to make – to Britain are out of all proportion to their numbers.

In 1066, for example, a small community of 5,000 French Jews were encouraged by King William I to bring their capital and financial skills to Britain. It became an indispensable source of finance for the King and the people. At the time, a law forbad Christians from lending money, and Jews were not allowed to do any other work so money-lending was the only profession they could enter. This led to Jewish people being the founders of banking and financial services in Britain.

From the 14th century, French weavers, German mining engineers, Dutch canal builders, printers, brewers and brickmakers brought new manufacturing skills and techniques at a time when wool was Britain's only major export.

Faced with the massive task of reconstruction after the Second World War, and acute labour shortages, the British government encouraged immigration, first from among European refugees displaced by the war, and then from Ireland and the Commonwealth. Before long, in some factories, mills and plants, the overwhelming majority of workers were Asian or black.

FROM WWW.CRE.ORG.UK/ETHDIV

Race in Britain: the last 50 years

1948 – The first West Indian immigrants come to Britain, invited by the British government to help with the shortage of unskilled workers.

1952 – Sprinter Emmanuel McDonald Bailey becomes the first black athlete to win an Olympic medal for Britain (100 metres).

1960 – India and Pakistan begin to issue passports to allow economic migration to Britain. In 1961, 48,850 people arrive from these countries.

1968–76 – Thousands of African Asians come from East Africa, many to escape the persecution of the dictator Idi Amin. Many bring useful business and professional skills.

1973 – Trevor McDonald becomes ITV's first black reporter.

1976 – The Race Relations Act is passed to promote racial equality and tackle discrimination. The Commission for Racial Equality is set up.

1979 – The first of 22,000 Vietnamese refugees arrive, fleeing Communism in Vietnam.

1980–81 – Race riots in Bristol and London.

1987 – Three black and one Asian MP are elected in the General Election.

1992 – The Maastricht Treaty is passed, allowing citizens of the European Union states to live and work in Britain.

1993 – Paul Ince becomes the first black player to captain England's football team.

2001 – Race riots in Oldham, Burnley, Stoke and Bradford.

2003 – Asylum seekers continue to seek a haven in Britain from persecution and war in countries such as Sri Lanka, Iraq and Afghanistan.

 ❶ Why could England be described as a 'melting pot'?

❷ Identify three different reasons why immigrant groups have come to Britain in the last 40,000 years. Are these the same reasons why different peoples are still coming to Britain today?

❸ Why is this ethnic immigration described as 'Britain's benefit'?

❹ Discuss why you think people coming to Britain are often met with hostility and resentment.

 On your own, choose one of the immigrant groups mentioned in the articles and find out more about their history. What reasons did they have for coming, and what did they contribute to Britain's culture?

 ❶ Study the timeline 'Race in Britain'. What do you learn from it about the main groups of immigrants that have come to Britain in the last 50 years?

❷ Use the information on these pages to extend this timeline backwards 40,000 years. Call it 'The Making of Britain'.

Is there a national identity and culture in Britain?

Aim: To explore the meaning of national identity and culture (Citizenship 1a, 2a, 2b, 2c)

What does 'being British' mean?

"You're only truly British if you were born in Britain."

"It means having a passport as a British citizen."

"It means speaking English and accepting the British way of life."

"It's got nothing to do with race or religion or cultural traditions. All sorts of people are British, because their families have chosen to live here."

"You're British if you've made your permanent home in the UK."

 Read what these young people have to say about being British. Discuss what being British means to you.

Tebbit's cricket loyalty test hit for six

A majority of black and Asian people in Britain see themselves as British, according to the first official figures on national identity published by the Office for National Statistics (ONS) in January 2004. Four out of every five people from the black Caribbean community living in Britain described their national identity as British, English, Scottish, Welsh or Irish. Three-quarters of the Indian, Pakistani and Bangladeshi communities identified themselves in the same way.

The figures may finally lay to rest suspicions among sections of the white majority whipped up by Lord Tebbit when he suggested in 1990 that immigrants and their children could not show loyalty to Britain until they supported the England team at cricket.

This attitude was further challenged by ONS data showing only 27% of people in Scotland described themselves as British, with the rest preferring to identify themselves as Scottish. In Wales 35% said they were British and 62% Welsh. Their loyalty to the England cricket team may also be questioned without accusing them of lack of patriotism.

The ethnicity report showed the group least likely to identify themselves as British were those recording themselves as 'other white', including Europeans and Americans. Less than 40% of this group said they were British, English, Scottish, Welsh or Irish.

The ONS said: "People from the white British group were more likely to describe their national identity as English, rather than British. However, the opposite was true of the non-white groups, who were far more likely to identify themselves as British."

FROM AN ARTICLE BY JOHN CARVEL, *THE GUARDIAN*

 ① Discuss this article. What is the main point that it is making?

② Why do you think ethnic minority groups identify themselves as British rather than English, Welsh or Scottish, etc?

FOR YOUR FILE

The government is considering testing prospective British citizens on knowledge of the history and culture of Britain, and on the English language. If they fail they would be barred from voting and not have passports. Write your views on whether or not you think this is a good idea.

Roots and branches

How do ethnic minority families manage to retain their heritage while living in Britain? Nadia Marks talks to three families with roots abroad:

Cecile Chukwumah is Nigerian. She lives in London with her two daughters, Nkechi, 10, and Chidera, nine

CECILE: "My identity is most definitely Nigerian. I was born in Nigeria and came to England when I was 13. I'm bringing up my girls to acknowledge their roots, but at the same time to appreciate the culture they are growing up in."

NKECHI: "I don't really feel any different to any of my school friends, apart from the way they speak to adults. We always call an adult 'auntie' or 'uncle' as a sign of respect, but they just call them by their first name and I think that's rude.

It's exciting being Nigerian because we have another country we can go and live in or visit. One of my friends at school is also Nigerian and we sang the Nigerian national anthem in assembly. Everyone clapped and I felt very proud."

Sunil and Parul Shah are Hindu, live in Milton Keynes and have two sons, Mayur, 14, and Tushar, 16

SUNIL: "My father emigrated from India to Africa, where I was born, and so did my wife's parents. Our parents managed to keep their ethnic identity and pass it on to us, so we are passing it on to our children. Our culture, language, religion and moral values are all important in identifying who, and what, we are.

It was important for us to marry a Hindu because we have the same values and are raising our children in agreement. But we understand the importance of adapting to western culture."

MAYUR: "When I was small I used to be embarrassed if my parents spoke to me in Gujarati, but now I am proud and very pleased to be able to communicate with my grandmother, who doesn't speak English. It gives me a sense of my culture and reminds me of who I am."

Roya and Hossein Shahidi are Iranians who live in London. They have two sons, Farhang, 15, and Farhad, 21

ROYA: "You cannot get away from who you are culturally, but given the choice you can create your own unique culture and be a more enriched person. We are Persian-Iranian and have a rich culture, such as our language, history, literature, music and food. These are all things we want to pass down to our children. I feel it is a blessing to be able to embrace two cultures, and it is beneficial not only to us as immigrants but to our host country, too. It is a two-way process."

FARHANG: "Being Iranian is not something that I consciously think about. I suppose I feel as British as I do Iranian because I fit into both cultures with the same ease. What does make me feel good, though, is the knowledge that I have this dual nationality. I know what it is like to be a foreigner in this country, but I also know what it is like being British."

FROM AN ARTICLE *'ROOTS AND BRANCHES'* BY NADIA MARKS, *THE GUARDIAN*

 1 Discuss what these families are saying about being part of more than one culture.

2 Do they identify with one culture more than the other?

3 Are the conflicting loyalties a burden or a benefit?

4 Do the children feel any differently from their parents?

"I'm a British African-Caribbean. My parents came to Britain from the West Indies before I was born. They're British West Indians."

"I'm from Glasgow. I'm Scottish and British."

"My parents are from Pakistan. I'm from Oldham. I suppose I'm a Lancastrian British Asian."

 Discuss what you think these young people are saying about their identity. How would you describe your own identity, and that of your family?

2 HUMAN RIGHTS

What are human rights and why do we have them?

Aim: To discuss what human rights are and which rights are most important
(Citizenship 1a, 2a, 2b, 2c)

What are human rights?

Human rights are a group of ideas. They are things that everyone is entitled to. Basic human rights include the right to life, and the right to food and clean drinking water. Others include the right to vote and to freedom of expression.

In the UK, most people have their basic human rights met. However, in some countries people's freedoms may be limited. And in the UK, there are still areas of human rights that some people believe could be improved, such as the rights of people with disabilities (see page 13).

Look at the photo above – what rights do you think are being violated here?

Where did human rights come from?

Modern human rights were developed after the Second World War, when many people's rights were violated. On a large scale, these human rights abuses are known as war crimes.

As a result, the United Nations (UN) was formed to provide a place for nations to resolve conflicts peacefully. The Universal Declaration of Human Rights (UDHR), consisting of 30 articles describing the basic rights of every person, was signed in 1948 by the 48 countries in the UN.

The first section of the Universal Declaration states:

'All human beings are born free and equal in dignity and rights'.

Key rights relating to being 'born free' include freedom of speech and of movement, the right to a fair trial, and freedom from torture and freedom from hunger.

Key rights relating to 'being equal' include a right to an education, and the right to be treated equally, without discrimination, in all areas of public life.

The Universal Declaration was designed as a safeguard to protect the human rights of people around the world. However, it has been criticised for being too weak because, as it is a Declaration, it cannot be enforced by law.

A legal basis for human rights

The European Convention of Human Rights was passed in 1963, giving a legal framework for human rights in the UK and other European countries. Here, people can complain to the European Court of Human Rights (ECHR), based in Strasbourg, France.

In 1998, the Human Rights Act was passed in the UK. It does several things:

- People can complain about human rights abuses in the UK courts, rather than having to go to Strasbourg.

- Existing laws in the UK must be interpreted as if they were compatible with the European Convention of Human Rights, and new laws must uphold human rights.

- In the UK, we now enjoy similar rights to other European countries, e.g. the right to practise a religion.

- In the case of a national emergency, however, or if one person's rights begin to violate another's, these rights are limited, e.g. in the event of a terrorist attack, people's freedom of movement can be restricted.

New human rights

In 1998, the European Union (EU) decided to update the list of human rights, to take account of changes in society and technology. The result was the European Charter of Fundamental Rights in 2000, which included some new human rights:

- The right to a private life, including a right to privacy and confidentiality of letters and emails.
- The right to limits on working hours and to have annual paid holiday.
- The right to respect the integrity of human beings, including a ban on financial gain from the human body, such as the sale of human organs and the cloning of human beings.
- The right to data protection, which means that if a company holds data on you, you can ask where they got the information and what the information is.

Human rights issues

In France, all schools are secular or non-religious. In 2003 the French government ruled that religious clothing would not be allowed in schools. However, many human rights activists have argued that this is discriminatory because Muslims, Sikhs and Jews would not be allowed to wear certain religious items. Under the Human Rights Act, this would restrict their 'right to practise a religion'.

In the UK, homosexuals are not allowed to serve in the military as some commanders think that this would make combat units less effective. The ECHR has ruled that this action violates the rights of homosexuals, who should be treated identically to everyone else.

 Discuss what you think about the French government's decision.

 Do you think that homosexuals should be allowed to serve in the military?

 There are a number of different groups that campaign on human rights in the UK. One such group, Liberty, aims to promote and extend human rights in the UK.

Which are the most important human rights to you? Why?

> "I would create a law outlawing abortion in the UK. Everyone's entitled to a right to life."
>
> *Anna, Belfast*

> "I would create a law making it free for everyone to go to University. Education should be right, not a privilege."
>
> *Dominic, Plymouth*

FOR YOUR FILE

If you could make one new law to enforce a new human right, what right would you choose and why? Give reasons.

The connection between rights and responsibilities

Aim: To discuss what responsibilities are and how they relate to human rights
(Citizenship 1a, 2a, 2b, 2c)

What are responsibilities?

Responsibilities are things that people have to do in order to protect each other's human rights. At 17, for example, you have the *right* to learn to drive a car to increase your freedom of movement. However, you also have the *responsibility* to drive safely and to obey the Highway Code.

 What rights and responsibilities do these travellers have?

How rights become responsibilities

The table shows three articles from the Universal Declaration of Human Rights (UDHR) and their key responsibilities.

Human right	Key responsibilities
Everyone should be treated in the same way and laws should apply equally to everyone. (Article 7)	We should treat everyone equally. It does not matter about a person's age, gender, race or religion.
Everyone is innocent until it can be proven that they are guilty. Everyone has the right to defend themselves at any public trial. (Article 11)	We must listen to both sides of an argument and not jump to conclusions. People should have a chance to explain themselves.
Everyone is entitled to privacy. (Article 12)	You should respect other people's privacy and they yours. No one may enter your house or read your mail without good reason.

① Look at the table above. Which do you think are the most important rights and responsibilities? Why?

② Draw up your own chart of rights and responsibilities, using different examples.

Freedom of speech – a conflict of rights

Antiracist campaigners say that the British National Party (BNP) should be denied freedom of speech. "This party supports racist ideas," said a spokesperson. "This goes against Article 7 of the UDHR, that 'everyone has the right to be treated equally'."

The BNP, however, claim they have a right to be heard under Article 19 – 'the right to freedom of speech' – and that this includes the BNP.

Do you think the BNP have the right to a freedom of speech, or should they be banned from TV and radio? Give reasons.

A group of schoolboys were punished for not stopping a fight. "We were told not to get involved, so we didn't", said one of the boys.

A teacher explained, "The boys were all crowded round so we couldn't reach the fighters. This meant we had to punish some boys in the crowd as well."

Do you think the boys in the crowd had a responsibility to stop the fight? Write a short statement saying what you think, giving reasons.

Equal opportunities

In order to achieve Article 7 of the UDHR, the UK government promotes the idea of equal opportunities. This means that everyone has an equal opportunity in life, including in employment, education and access to services.

Disability rights in the UK

A disability is an impairment or medical condition that prevents someone from doing something. Physical impairments include hearing difficulties, vision impairment or mobility problems, such as being unable to walk without assistance. Other impairments, such as a learning difficulties, restrict a person's mental development.

A wide variety of human rights exist to protect people with disabilities. Article 22 of the UDHR states that, 'Everyone, as a member of society, is entitled to realisation of their economic, social and cultural rights'. This means that we, as individuals and as a society, have a responsibility to help people with disabilities lead as normal a life as possible.

The Disability Discrimination Act 1995

This Act means that everyone has the responsibility not to discriminate against people with disabilities with regards to:

- access to goods, facilities, and services
- employment
- the management, buying or renting of land or property.

From 2004, businesses have had to make reasonable changes to their properties to accommodate people with disabilities, including:

- access ramps for people in wheelchairs
- hearing loops for those who find it difficult to hear
- colour-coding in large buildings, such as hospitals, for people whose vision is impaired.

"People with disabilities have responsibilities too, to tell us how we can help them. And they should be treated equally, not better than the rest of us."

Duncan, Edinburgh

❶ Look at the three statements. Do you agree or disagree? Why?

❷ How would a person with a physical disability that restricts their mobility, e.g. a wheelchair user, cope in your local area? Suggest what could be done to improve the local situation.

"The problem is, people look at me in a wheelchair and think I can't do anything. But the fact is that I love canoeing and snooker. I should be given the option to decide what I can and can't do."

Amanda, Liverpool

"It's the simple things that make a difference. All traffic lights bleep to help partially-sighted people like myself cross the road safely. The council or the government should do more to help people with disabilities."

Paul, Bournemouth

3 RIGHTS AND RESPONSIBILITIES

Parents and young people

Aim: To explore the rights and responsibilities of people at home and at school
(Citizenship 1a, 2a, 2b, 2c)

Parental responsibility

'Parental responsibility' describes the rights and responsibilities that parents have towards their children. Until their child reaches 16, parents are responsible for:

- looking after them
- feeding and clothing them
- making decisions about their schooling
- agreeing to medical treatment
- making decisions about where they should live.

Although the Children Act (1989) defined the idea of parental responsibility, it only gives general guidelines – that parents must protect the under-16s from harm. But what is harmful? That is up to the parent's judgement. Social Services would only get involved if they felt that a child was at risk of suffering 'significant harm'.

Parents should make their decisions based on the age, maturity and wishes of the child. As Katy Macfarlane of the Scottish Child Law Centre says, "The key consideration when deciding to leave a child alone is whether you feel they are mature enough to know what to do in an emergency, such as a fire, and to follow your instructions if, say, someone comes to the door."

 1 Discuss parental responsibilities. Is it a good idea that the law leaves so much to the judgement of the parents?

2 If the law laid down strict ages for leaving children on their own, what ages would you give?

3 There is no law that states the age at which young people can baby-sit, but child charities recommend that the minimum age of a babysitter should be 16. Do you agree? Would you want to take any other factors into consideration?

 Which are the two most important rights and the two most important responsibilities in the table on page 15?

Rights and responsibilities at school

Rights		Responsibilities
• To choose the school for their child • To educate their child out of school	PARENTS	• To ensure their child goes to school • To ensure their child is suitably educated between the ages of five and 16
• To leave school at 16 • To be educated until they are 19	STUDENTS	• To obey school rules • To behave sensibly and reasonably
• To punish students, if reasonable cause • To confiscate certain items from students	TEACHERS	• To look after the students in their care as if they were parents (in *loco parentis*)
• To insist that their students wear uniform, if reasonable • To exclude students as a last resort for bad behaviour	SCHOOLS	• To take steps to prevent bullying • To provide students with religious and sex education

Growing up under the law

As you grow up, your right to do things varies according to how old you are and what it is you want to do. Here are some of the areas:

Smoking and buying cigarettes

It is not actually against the law for a child to smoke, but it is illegal to buy cigarettes before the age of 16. It is also illegal for shops to sell cigarettes to children under 16.

Buying and using drugs

If a child buys or is given an illegal drug, he or she can be arrested and charged with possession of drugs, or with supplying drugs, from the age of 10.

Going to the pub and drinking

Children under 14 will be refused entry to a bar. Children cannot buy and drink alcohol in a bar until they are 18. However, there is no law prohibiting children drinking alcohol at home from the age of five.

Gambling

Anyone under 18 is not allowed into a betting shop. No one under 16 is allowed to buy a lottery ticket.

Tattooing

It is an offence to tattoo anyone under the age of 18, except for medical reasons.

Sexual relationships

The age of consent for heterosexual relationships is 16, and 18 for homosexual relationships.

Contraception

Young people can obtain contraceptive advice and treatment without their parent's consent. Doctors can also provide advice and treatment to under-16s, if they believe that that person has sufficient maturity and understands the advice.

Marriage

A young person can get married at 16 with the consent of his or her parents. Once a person reaches the age of 18, he or she can get married without parental consent.

Learning to drive

A young person can obtain a licence for a moped from the age of 16, and for a motorbike from the age of 17. A young person can get a provisional driving licence for a car from the age of 17.

ADAPTED FROM NFPI LEAFLET '*IS IT LEGAL?*', PGS 15–16

① **Draw a timeline from age 0 to 21 and mark on it at what age you are allowed to do the things listed in the article above.**

② **Research the age restrictions of some of the activities that have not been included, such as voting, joining the armed forces, becoming an MP, driving a heavy goods vehicle, or buying a pet. Add them to your timeline.**

FOR YOUR FILE

Are there any entries in your timeline that you disagree with? Choose one or more and write a paragraph explaining what the law is on these issues, why you think the law has been passed, and what your objections to it are.

Employers and workers

Aim: To explore the rights and responsibilities of people at work (Citizenship 1h, 2a, 2b, 2c)

What is work?

Although most workers are employed full time, there are many different patterns of work. There are permanent and temporary jobs. Part-time work has increased, with nearly as many women working part-time compared to those that work full time. Or people to choose to be self-employed, which means they do not have an employer, but they sell their labour directly to the customer. This can mean hard work and long hours, but the possibility of greater freedom, working independently.

As a result of modern technology, more office jobs are being done at home (teleworking). There's also voluntary work – people working in the community for charities, hospitals and schools, etc., who earn no money but who improve the quality of other people's lives. This is the same for unpaid work in the home, such as caring, cooking and housework.

 Discuss what counts as work in today's society. Write down one example of each of the different working patterns listed above. What are the advantages and disadvantages of each? What is their value to society?

Starting work

If you are employed for more than a month, you must have a contract with your employer. The contract lists the terms and conditions of employment, i.e. the responsibilities that you have, as well as your right to pay, holidays, etc. The contract can be agreed verbally, but employees have the right to a written statement of the main terms of employment within two months of starting work. This statement should give:

- your job title and place of work
- your starting date
- details of how much you will be paid, and when
- your hours of work
- your holiday entitlement
- arrangements for sick pay and pension
- details of how complaints at work are dealt with
- the amount of notice you and your employer must give to end the contract.

FOR YOUR FILE

A friend has written to say that they have started a new job, but have not received a contract. Write to them explaining why you think it is important for them to have a contract and what the contract should include.

The law at work

A number of laws protect the rights of employees and ensure equal opportunities at work. Here are five of the most important laws.

Equal Pay Act 1970

If you are a woman, you are entitled to the same pay as a man doing the same (or similar) job, or a job of equal value. The Act covers all pay, i.e. bonuses, holiday pay, sick pay and pensions, as well as wages and salaries. It covers full-time, part-time and temporary workers.

Health and Safety Act 1974

Employers have a legal duty to take care of the health of their staff. This means that the equipment that you use must not be dangerous or defective, and that the people you work with must work safely and responsibly. Your duty is to follow safety regulations, and to take care of your own and other people's safety.

Sex Discrimination Acts 1975 and 1986

It is unlawful to treat you, on the grounds of your sex, less favourably than a person of the opposite sex. Not employing someone because she is a woman is direct discrimination. Applying conditions for a job which favour one sex over another (e.g. asking for workers who are over 1.7m tall) is indirect discrimination: both are illegal.

Race Relations Act 1976

It is unlawful to discriminate against you because of your race, colour, country of origin, nationality or ethnic group. The Commission for Racial Equality gives advice and information on racial matters, and supports those who believe they have been discriminated against, whether in the workplace or any other public sphere.

Disability Discrimination Act 1995

If you are disabled, you cannot be treated less favourably than any other employee in terms of recruitment, pay, promotion, or any other terms of employment. This Act applies to firms of 20 or more employees. The Disability Rights Commission supports those who feel they have been discriminated against because of their disability.

Tribunals

Many disputes at the workplace go to an employment tribunal. This is a kind of court which hears both the employer's and the employee's side of the argument. If the applicant wins the case, they are usually awarded a sum of money (called compensation).

 Discuss the rights and responsibilities of employers and employees. Why do we need employment laws? Do workers have responsibilities as well as rights?

❶ Choose one of the five main laws passed to protect employees' rights and investigate it further on the internet. For further information, visit:
- the Equal Opportunities Commission: www.eoc.org.uk
- the Disability Rights Commission: www.drc-gb.org
- the Commission for Racial Equality: www.cre.gov.uk.

❷ Prepare a presentation to contribute to a class debate on which is the most important employment law.

Consumers and traders

Your rights when shopping

Consumers may be shopping for goods (i.e. buying items) or for services (i.e. buying a skill such as a haircut or professional advice from a plumber). Either way they make a contract with the trader, which is legally binding in civil law (see page 20). If the goods or services supplied are faulty or inadequate, your rights are protected by law.

When buying goods...	When buying a service...
Under the Sale of Goods Act, the law states that the goods must be: ● **of satisfactory quality** – taking into account the description and price ● **fit for their purpose** – they must do what the seller and manufacturer says they can do ● **as described** – they must fit the description on the package or display sign, or that given by the seller. This law applies also to second-hand goods, goods in a sale or bought by mail order, over the phone or on the internet. It does not apply to goods bought privately. In this case, the seller must not mislead you and must describe the goods correctly.	Under the Supply of Goods and Services Act, a service must be provided: ● **with reasonable care and skill** – the job should be done to a proper standard of workmanship ● **within a reasonable time** – even if you haven't agreed a definite completion date with the supplier of the service ● **for a reasonable charge** – unless you agreed a price beforehand. (An 'estimate' tells you roughly what the cost will be. A 'quotation' tells you the exact price and it is part of the contract between you and the supplier.) 'Reasonable' means compared with the normal standard, e.g. what you would normally expect from a plumber, etc.

Civil and criminal laws

The Sale of Goods Act and the Supply of Goods and Services Act are civil laws. There are also some criminal laws that protect the consumer.

● **The Trades Description Act** says that it is illegal to make a false description about goods or services.

● **The Consumer Protection Act** says that it is illegal to sell unsafe goods or to mislead consumers about the price of goods. The manufacturer or importer is liable for any loss or damage caused.

● **The Food Safety Act** says that it is illegal to sell food that doesn't comply with food safety requirements.

FOR YOUR FILE

The Ethical Consumer is a consumer organisation that investigates the social and environmental records of big brand names, and advises consumers to 'buy ethically'. Investigate one of the companies listed on www.ethicalconsumer.org and write a paragraph explaining why it is an ethical company to buy from.

When you have a complaint

Take the faulty item back to the shop as soon as possible and ask, firmly but politely, for a refund or for it to be exchanged. But what if the trader keeps arguing – what are your rights?

"It isn't our fault the goods are defective – go back to the manufacturer."

Not true – you bought the goods from the trader, not the manufacturer, and the trader is liable for any breaches of contract.

"You must produce your receipt."

Not true – in fact, the trader doesn't have to give you a receipt in the first place. However, it might be reasonable for the shop to want some proof of purchase, such as a credit card receipt or bank statement.

"We don't give any refunds – you must accept a credit note."

It depends. If you have changed your mind, the shop doesn't have to do anything. But if the goods are faulty, incorrectly described or not fit for their normal purpose, you are entitled to your money.

"No refunds can be given on sale items."

It depends on why you want to return them. The Sale of Goods Act still applies, but you won't be entitled to anything if you knew of any faults before purchase, if the fault should have been obvious to you or if you simply changed your mind.

"You only have rights for 30 days after purchase."

Not true – depending on circumstances. You might be too late to have all your money back after this time, but the trader will still be liable for any breaches of contract, such as the goods being faulty.

When are you not entitled to anything?

- If you were told of any faults before you bought the goods.
- If the fault was obvious and you should have noticed it before buying.
- If you caused any damage yourself.
- If you made a mistake, e.g. about the colour/size.
- If you have changed your mind about the goods or you have seen them cheaper elsewhere.
- If you bought the goods more than six years ago.

SLIGHTLY ADAPTED FROM WWW.TRADINGSTANDARDS.GOV.UK

 Write three true and three false statements about consumer rights. Ask your partner to identify which are which.

 Plan a radio phone-in consumer affairs programme. The theme of the programme is consumer rights. One of you is the presenter and four of you are experts on the panel. Be prepared to present a programme in front of the class, and to receive questions from the 'studio audience'.

4 THE LAW OF THE LAND

Explaining what the law means

What is the law?

In an ideal world we would act exactly as we pleased. Unfortunately, many of the things we want to do clash with, or affect, other people. Societies have therefore developed complex systems of regulating (or controlling) people's behaviour.

Here's the deal: the law restricts your behaviour in return for protecting you. It imposes 'responsibilities' because it demands that you behave in a certain way. But it also provides you with 'rights': you will be backed up by the State if these rights are infringed by others.

There are many aspects to the concept of 'law':

Custom and morality:
We are taught customs and morality from an early age. We follow custom when we take our place at the back of a queue or offer a visitor a drink. The moral values of communities are often based on religious ideas, such as the Koran for Muslims.

Law: A set of rules that regulate the relationships between people, between states, and between the people and the state. These rules are enforceable in the courts.

Rules and regulations:
Institutions – such as schools, businesses, train companies, and even the home – can draw up their own set of rules, but which cannot be backed up by the courts. These rules help things to run smoothly.

International law: Aimed at settling disputes between nations over such things as where they can trade or what weapons they can have. International law comes from treaties agreed between nations.

National law: The law that applies within a particular country. Laws passed by the British parliament apply to the whole of the UK. However, laws passed by the Scottish Parliament apply to Scotland only.

Public law: Public law relates to the state in some way, for example detailing the method of government. The most important type of public law is 'criminal law'.

Private law: Private law, or 'civil law', states what your duties and rights are in your dealings with other people.

Making the law

The law of England and Wales is a system that has developed over hundreds of years from various sources and is still developing today. The two main sources of law are common law and statute law.

The image of a female holding a sword in one hand and scales in the other is a universally recognised symbol of justice – an image that goes back to antiquity.

Common law	Statute law	Other sources of law
In the Middle Ages, judges decided important cases by following what was the local custom. This slowly formed the body of what is now called 'Common law' (because it was common to all areas of the country). Most civil law, and a lot of criminal law, is common law. Common law is an unwritten law based on the decisions of judges and is not defined by an Act of Parliament. When a judge makes a decision, it is based on the past decisions (precedents) of judges in similar cases. If a point of law has not already been decided, the judge will set a new precedent for the future.	When a government is formed after a general election, it has a series of reforms that it wants to carry out. This is done mainly by passing laws through Parliament. Laws may also be passed to deal with unforeseen events, for example new antiterrorism laws after the attack on the USA on 11 September 2002. Laws passed by Parliament are called Acts of Parliament, or statutes. They are proposed by the government as Bills and have to pass through several stages in both Houses of Parliament (see page 30) before they become law.	Sometimes Parliament authorises laws to be made by another person or body. Local by-laws, for example, are passed by local authorities. As Britain is a member of the European Union (EU), all EU treaties automatically become part of English law. Also, the European Parliament can pass new laws as either regulations or directives. Regulations become law automatically in member states; directives tell these states to pass their own laws to bring the directive into effect within a given time frame. European law has supremacy over the laws of any member country.

 ① Discuss what you have learned about the different ways in which laws are made.

② Should judges make the law in common law cases? What are the advantages and disadvantages of this kind of law?

③ Parliament is now the main law-making body in the UK. Why do you think that is?

 Discuss why you think most people obey the law. Is it because they have strong religious or moral principles or because they are afraid of being caught and punished? Or is there some other reason?

FOR YOUR FILE

Write a short article on 'Law' for an encyclopedia aimed at teenagers. You will need to explain clearly what law is and why it exists, and list two or three different types of law.

Civil law and criminal law

Aim: To explore the two main branches of national law, as well as the court system and the different professions who work in the law (Citizenship 1a, 2a, 2b, 2c)

	Civil law (private law)	Criminal law (public law)
Definition	Civil law states what your rights and duties are in your dealings with other people.	Criminal law deals with offences that everyone would agree are wrong. These actions are regarded as offences against *the State*, even though people are often the victims.
Examples	Disputes over contracts, property rights, discrimination, trespass, marriage, divorce.	Murder, violence, misuse of drugs, driving offences, fraud.
Purpose	To defend the rights of individuals and settle matters between them.	To protect society and the citizens of the state, and maintain law and order.
In court	The *claimant* takes action against (or sues) the *defendant* in a County Court. A judge decides whether the defendant is *liable* or not. If liable, the defendant usually has to pay *damages* to the claimant, or has an injunction taken out against them.	The *defendant is prosecuted* by the Crown. Most criminal cases are heard in a Magistrates' Court. Defendants are found guilty or not guilty; if guilty they are punished by fines, a community sentence or imprisonment.

The court system

Criminal and civil laws use a different system of courts. The courts higher up the pyramid (below) hear the more important or serious cases. They also hear appeals from decisions made in the lower courts. At the top of the diagram, the courts combine and can pass judgement in both civil and criminal cases.

The purple boxes relate to civil law, the blue7 boxes to criminal law. Dotted arrows show the appeal routes.

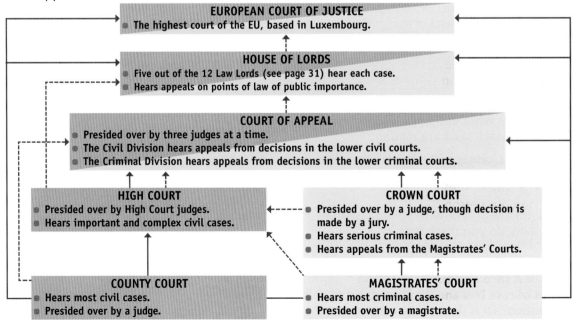

EUROPEAN COURT OF JUSTICE
- The highest court of the EU, based in Luxembourg.

HOUSE OF LORDS
- Five out of the 12 Law Lords (see page 31) hear each case.
- Hears appeals on points of law of public importance.

COURT OF APPEAL
- Presided over by three judges at a time.
- The Civil Division hears appeals from decisions in the lower civil courts.
- The Criminal Division hears appeals from decisions in the lower criminal courts.

HIGH COURT
- Presided over by High Court judges.
- Hears important and complex civil cases.

CROWN COURT
- Presided over by a judge, though decision is made by a jury.
- Hears serious criminal cases.
- Hears appeals from the Magistrates' Courts.

COUNTY COURT
- Hears most civil cases.
- Presided over by a judge.

MAGISTRATES' COURT
- Hears most criminal cases.
- Presided over by a magistrate.

People in the law

There are two kinds of lawyers in England and Wales – solicitors and barristers.

Solicitors

● Advise clients on a range of legal matters, such as drawing up a business contract, buying a house and making a will.

● Most work for a firm of solicitors, some of which specialise in particular areas of law.

● Since 2000, solicitors have been allowed to speak for their clients in the lower law courts.

 ① Discuss what you have learned about the English legal system.

② Write 10 questions about the law and test your partner with a quiz.

Barristers

● Will be contacted by a solicitor on behalf of the client if the case is serious. Barristers specialise in presenting cases in court (called advocacy) and mainly work in the higher law courts. They also give advice and draft documents.

● Barristers are self-employed, but they work as a unit which is collectively known as 'the Bar'.

FORMER Midchester and England footballer Lewis Safiri received a 12-month driving ban and a £400 fine when he appeared before a York Magistrates' Court today. He admitted driving while being drunk.

REM guitarist Peter Buck thanked the jury at Isleworth Crown Court after being cleared of going on a drunken rampage aboard a British Airways plane.

FAMILY doctor Patrick Vinall saw his career end in shame when a jury convicted him of two indecent assaults. The former GP was given two 18-month suspended sentences at Sheffield Crown Court.

MOTHER of five Sasha Clarke celebrated after a High Court judge ordered Milton Mowbray Hospital to pay her £50,000 in damages. Mrs Clarke had sued the hospital for negligence after she had lost her unborn child in a bungled operation.

 Read the news summaries above. Discuss each case and then answer the following questions.

① What caused the case to be brought to court?

② Which type of court dealt with it?

③ Who was the defendant?

④ Was it a civil or criminal case?

⑤ Who decided the verdict, and what decision was made?

 Choose one of these situations:

● A famous person believes that a newspaper has falsely accused her of having an affair.
● The police charge a man with murdering his wife.
● A young man is caught breaking and entering a house.

Invent some details for your case and prepare a presentation – either as role play, a cartoon strip or a transcript of part of the court proceedings for your case. Explain what kind of case it is and what happened when it reached the courts.

5 CRIME AND PUNISHMENT

Crime and young people

Aim: To explore how crime relates to young people, focusing on antisocial behaviour
(Citizenship 1a, 2a, 2b, 2c)

Criminal responsibility

In law, you have to be a certain age before you are regarded as fully responsible for your actions. This is called the 'age of criminal responsibility'. This means that in England and Wales, you cannot be charged with a criminal offence until you are 10 years old. When you are 10, however, the courts will assume that you knew what you were doing when you committed a crime.

The age of criminal responsibility is controversial. Here are two views:

> "I think that at 14 years old, children are better able to understand the consequences of what they are doing. A child of 10 who has committed an offence is more appropriately dealt with in the care system than in the criminal justice system. The European Court says that a child must be able to participate in their own defence, and I think a child of 14 is able to do that but a child of 10 is not."
>
> Carolyn Hamilton, Director of the Children's Legal Centre, who wants the age of criminal responsibility raised to 14.

> "Children of 10 know the difference between right and wrong. They know you don't hurt small children. We have children as young as eight, or even six, terrorising people on estates such as the one I live on. I also think parents should be held responsible for their children's behaviour."
>
> Lyn Costello, Mothers Against Murder and Aggression, who wants the age lowered to eight years old.

Discuss what you think the age of criminal responsibility should be. Think about these questions:

1. **Do children understand the consequences of their actions?**
2. **Should children be dealt with by the care system or the criminal system?**
3. **Is a child able to participate in his or her own defence?**
4. **Should parents be responsible for their child's behaviour?**

Antisocial behaviour

A day in the life of yob-culture Britain

by Philip Johnston, Home Affairs Editor for the *Telegraph*

On 10 September 2003, 66,000 incidents of rowdiness, intimidation, littering, drunkenness, drug-taking and vandalism were reported to various public agencies – that's more than one every two seconds.

The highest number of reports was generated by people dropping litter or dumping rubbish, vandalism, rowdiness and nuisance behaviour. There were nearly 5,000 complaints about abandoned vehicles and more than 6,000 about drunkenness and drug-taking.

The figures were gathered in the first census of antisocial behaviour in England and Wales. They provided the backdrop for a renewed Government effort to get to grips with the problem, headed by the Prime Minister.

Brighton, Bristol, Leeds, and the London borough of Camden and city of Westminster will clamp down on begging, while London and Liverpool will try to clear away abandoned cars. Other areas, still to be identified, will be targeted for a '100 days clean-up' programme, attacking local priorities, such as removing abandoned cars or graffiti.

The initiative will also try to clear away thousands of abandoned vehicles. Last year, 300,000 cars were dumped. Another project will close off dark and dangerous alleyways often used as escape routes by criminals.

Ministers argue that neighbourhoods blighted by vandals feel and look unsafe and encourage criminals and drug dealers to move in. However, the principal reason the yobs have taken over is because the police are less often seen on the streets. Mr Blunkett said he wanted to find out why there are 36,000 more police today than 30 years ago, yet fewer than ever are seen on patrol.

Jan Berry, the Chairman of the Police Federation, said: "It's extremely frustrating for police to try to remove some of these young people from the streets when they then see them going straight back and no real sanctions are taking place."

FROM WWW.TELEGRAPH.CO.UK/NEWS

 ❶ Which kinds of behaviour noted in the article do you think are the most antisocial? Are there any others that you would add?

❷ What attempts is the Government making to tackle antisocial behaviour? Will it be successful?

❸ In the article, three reasons for antisocial behaviour are given: run-down neighbourhoods, fewer police officers and no real sanctions. What do *you* think the main reasons are?

❹ In the article, Jan Berry identifies those responsible as 'young people'. Do you agree?

 ❶ You are members of a local committee deciding what to do in order to reduce antisocial behaviour locally. Which of these do you think would be most effective?

- Provide more clubs and facilities for young people.
- Use tougher sanctions for antisocial behaviour, e.g. curfews or antisocial behaviour orders.
- Increase the number of police patrols.
- Close pubs that serve alcohol to under-age drinkers.
- Set up youth action groups to involve young people in schemes to improve the neighbourhood.

❷ What other actions would you recommend?

Aim: To explore the work of the police and the criminal justice system
(Citizenship 1a, 2a, 2b, 2c)

USING NEW TOOLS TO ATTACK THE ROOTS OF CRIME

The role of the police has moved far beyond that of the traditional copper displayed in the 1950s TV series, *Dixon of Dock Green*, as Nick Davies reports

Consider the case of the car park in the country. Ramblers used to turn up, park their cars, head off on a hike and then return to find their car windows smashed and their belongings stolen. George Dixon's answer would have been to get out his handcuffs, hide behind a bush until the thieves turned up, nick them and wobble off home on his bicycle. In the real world, another thief would have been breaking into the cars before he reached Dock Green and the offenders he arrested would have been bailed to join in again the next day.

For decades, British police would have been happy enough with that failure: they had no option. But in the past 20 years researchers in the United States and Britain have been urging them to think in a radically different way – to stop relying on the conventional tools of arrest and conviction, and to start looking beneath the surface to manipulate the causes of crime, to stop being dragged around by events in favour of stepping back and trying to change them. They call it 'problem-oriented policing'.

In the case of the car park, instead of reaching for their handcuffs, the local police stopped and analysed the crime. They realised that the real problem was simply that once the ramblers hit the hills there was nothing and nobody to stop the thieves doing exactly as they pleased. So they decided to solve the problem at its root – by building picnic tables at the side of the car park. To make sure that picnickers turned up, they arranged for a licensed vendor to sell drink and food up

Friendly copper, Dixon of Dock Green, from the 1950s TV series

A modern-day police officer

there. Natural surveillance. They cut the thieving by 48% in a year.

This problem-oriented approach is the heart of a far wider effort to bury George Dixon: to say that arrests and convictions have their uses but they also have their limits; to work with other agencies and deliver something other than punishment; to attack the infinitely complex roots of crime with infinitely flexible tactics. It's not so much criminal justice as crime reduction.

FROM *THE GUARDIAN*

❶ **Discuss what you have learned about different methods of policing.**

❷ **Do you think it is the job of the police to prevent crime as much as to detect it?**

❸ **How else, other than arrests, can these problems be tackled?**

● A spate of muggings along a dark alleyway leading to a housing estate.

● Regular drunken gatherings outside a pizza parlour where there are too many people queuing for their pizzas on Friday nights after the pub closes.

FOR YOUR FILE

Research the job of the Community Support Officers who were brought in to help the police in 2003.

The process of youth justice

If you are arrested by the police and are 10–17 years old, you can expect the following to happen:

1. The police station	2. The Youth Court
The duty officer must find your parent or guardian to be present when you are charged with an offence. They may also instruct a solicitor on your behalf. If you admit to the offence, you may be issued with a warning. After two warnings, you will be sent to court. If your offence is serious, there will be no warnings: you will be sent to court and prosecuted. 	A Youth Court is a special kind of Magistrates' Court (see page 22), where the procedure is less formal. You must be accompanied by your parent or guardian if you are under 16. (Only if the offence is very serious will you be sent to a Crown Court.) A clerk asks if the defendant (you) pleads guilty or not guilty. If guilty, the prosecutor (person charging you) outlines the facts of the case, and the magistrates decide on the sentence after taking into account any special factors that could lead to a lesser sentence. If you plead not guilty, there must be a trial. If, at the end of the trial, the magistrates find you guilty, your sentence will be harsher. If found not guilty, then you are free to go.

People in the English courts

Magistrates – about 30,000 magistrates deal with over 98% of criminal cases. They are unpaid and have no formal qualifications, although they are advised by a legally-qualified court clerk.

Judges – in the criminal justice system, judges hear only 2% of the most serious cases. All judges are appointed by the Lord Chancellor and must be qualified barristers or solicitors (see page 23).

Juries – in England, juries consist of 12 adults chosen at random from the electoral register. The jury decides whether a defendant in a Crown Court is innocent or guilty. They are advised by the judge before they come to their verdict. Trial by jury is regarded as one of the strengths of the English justice system, although the government has suggested restricting jury trials in many cases.

"Jury trials are an expensive waste as juries often make the wrong decision."

"Trial by jury is a time-honoured way of ensuring that a person gets a fair trial."

"A judge has seen it all before – whereas a jury hasn't – and is far more likely to reach the right decision because a judge knows the law."

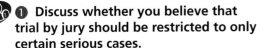 **1** Discuss whether you believe that trial by jury should be restricted to only certain serious cases.

2 Role play the case of a young person who has been caught stealing a car and has been arrested for the first time.

FOR YOUR FILE

Write an article on the system of trial by jury for an encyclopedia for teenagers. Include a short history, an explanation of how the system works, and a summary of any controversial issues. Visit www.cjsonline.org for more information.

Punishment and sentencing

Aim: To explore the kinds of sentencing available to the courts, focusing especially on the use of prisons (Citizenship 1a, 2a, 2b, 2c)

Sentencing

A sentence is the punishment imposed on someone who has been found guilty in a criminal court. Except in murder cases (when a life sentence is automatic) and a few other cases, the judge or magistrates can choose a sentence from a wide range.

The sentence always depends on all the circumstances of the particular case and of the person involved. In many cases the law states maximum or minimum sentences or fines, but within these limits there is a large measure of choice.

The main choices are:
- **A custodial sentence:** Sending the offender to prison, a young offender institution, a secure training centre, or to an accommodation centre.
- **Fining the offender**, ordering them to pay compensation to the victim, or both. The amount of the fine or compensation will depend on how much money the offender has.
- **An order controlling the conduct or activity of the offender**, e.g. a drug rehabilitation programme, regular reporting to a probation officer or to the Youth Offending Team, undertaking some form of community punishment or unpaid community work, or going to an attendance centre.
- **A parenting order:** The courts can make orders for those who are responsible for under-18s, to help the parent or guardian control the activities of the young person.

The main reasons behind choosing the different types of sentence are:
- **to protect others** – prison makes sure that the offender can't commit any crimes
- **to help the offender** – training and activities encourage them to 'go straight'
- **to punish the offender** – some crimes may deserve a strong punishment
- **to deter the offender and others** from doing the same thing again
- **to give something back to society or to the victim** for what they have suffered.

FROM 'RUNNING A MOCK TRIAL', WWW.CITIZENSHIPFOUNDATION.ORG.UK

1 Discuss and list the advantages and disadvantages of custodial and alternative sentences.

2 Look at the cases below. Match the cases to the sentences and explain your reasons.

Case 1
Paul, 25, was part of a gang of football supporters that ran riot in a pub. Three people were injured. No one actually saw Paul attack the individuals. Paul was found guilty of 'causing an affray'. The judge was told that Paul had three previous convictions for violence at football matches.

Case 2
Three 16-year-old girls attacked a woman, injured her, and stole her bag and watch. None of the girls had a previous conviction. The judge wanted the girls to learn a lesson.

Case 3
Laurence, 12, admitted stealing property worth £3,000. Another 78 offences were 'taken into account'. He was thought to have stolen about £10,000 worth of goods, passing them on to adults.

Sentences

A Six years in prison

B Conditional discharge (if offender commits another offence within a certain time, they go back to court to be sentenced for both offences)

C A fine and an order to pay compensation

D Taken into the care of the local authority

Barring the way

Statistics and experience tells us that prisons aren't working, says Lucie Russell, Director of the Smart Justice Campaign

Prison isn't working. Around three-quarters of young offenders and half of all offenders commit another crime within two years of release, at a cost of around £11 billion to the taxpayer; and it costs £37,500 to keep one prisoner in jail for a year – that's a lot to pay for a failing public service.

It is true to say that offenders cannot commit crimes while they are behind bars, but it is worth remembering that all but a handful of offenders are released into the community, and that the majority of them re-offend. Of course, prisons are necessary. We need them to keep us safe from violent and serious offenders. But they do not turn people into respectable, law-abiding citizens. Offenders – most of whom are imprisoned for non-violent crimes – emerge from jail hardened, alienated and ill-equipped for life outside. They are also armed with fresh criminal contacts and skills.

It's been proved that community-based programmes for non-violent offenders are more effective at cutting crime than prison, and are a fraction of the cost. Of every 100 people who serve a community sentence, 11 fewer are reconvicted within two years compared with those who are imprisoned. Community programmes deserve more money and resources, so that they can be delivered consistently throughout the country. It makes sense to tackle non-serious crime in the community, while at the same time freeing up prison space for dangerous criminals.

FROM 'BARRING THE WAY TO SUCCESS', BIG ISSUE

"Prison worked for me," says Lee, 22

"I never want to go back there again," says Lee, who was jailed for 18 months. "I got drunk and was involved in a brawl. It's really tough losing your freedom. I spent most of the day locked in a cell with a person I'd never have spoken to outside. People who say prison isn't a deterrent don't know what they're talking about. It's humiliating and degrading, but at least I got the opportunity to do some training, and I've now got myself a better job than I had before. But basically prison was hell. I'm determined I'll never, ever go there again."

Discuss whether you think prison is a bad way of punishing criminals. Or do you agree with Lee that prison works?

6 IT'S YOUR GOVERNMENT

The UK Parliament

Aim: To understand what the UK Parliament is and what it does (Citizenship 1c, 1d, 2a, 2b, 2c)

What is the UK Parliament?

There are three parts of the UK Parliament – the House of Commons, the House of Lords, and the monarchy (see page 35).

The origins of Parliament lie in medieval times. When the monarch needed to raise large amounts of money, nobles formed a Great Council (later the House of Lords). The Great Council also consisted of local people – commoners (later the House of Commons).

At this time, the monarch held absolute power. Over time, power has transferred from the monarch to the House of Commons. However, some power is held by the House of Lords.

What the UK Parliament does

Parliament has several different functions:

Most laws are passed by the UK Parliament in Westminster. However, local councils can pass minor, local laws ('by-laws').

To scrutinise and debate laws that are passed in Europe. More and more decisions are made in Europe, with legal force across the European Union (EU) (see page 20).

To agree a budget, which includes the income and expenditure for the government each year, and to scrutinise how this money is spent.

To debate major, current issues of political importance.

 Look at the different functions of Parliament. Which do you think are the most important? Give reasons for your views.

When does the UK Parliament meet?

Parliament starts immediately after a general election has been called and can last up to five years. However, as the Prime Minister decides when a general election is called, an average Parliament lasts four years.

The parliamentary year starts in either October or November. There are gaps in a year where Parliament does not 'sit' (meet). These are known as adjournments. These include public holidays and a summer holiday.

 Do you think it is right that the Prime Minister decides when we have a general election?

How Parliament works

Parliament follows a set of rules known as 'standing orders'. These control the order in which people make speeches, interrupt a speaker, and how a debate is run. Each debate has a 'motion'. For example, a motion on fox hunting might read, 'This house believes that fox hunting should be banned, and calls on the Government to introduce a new law, known as a Bill, to achieve this'.

At the end of a debate, a vote is taken. If there is no general agreement the motion is passed if it has a majority of votes.

However, voting in both Houses of Parliament is done by a traditional method where people walk through one corridors for 'yes' and one for 'no'. Some say that this is an important tradition, allowing time for politicians to discuss business while queuing to walk through either door. Others argue that electronic voting should be used – it is more efficient and less time-consuming – but the current chamber is too small for this.

 Should there be electronic voting in the House of Commons and a new modernised chamber? Or should we keep the current system? Give reasons for your views.

The House of Commons

There are 659 members of the House of Commons, including the leaders of all the main political parties. In 2004, these members included 120 women, and 12 MPs who were from ethnic minorities. However, both groups are still significantly under-represented.

The House of Commons has 15 select committees, made up of 10–20 MPs, who look at one specific area of parliamentary business. For example, the work of the Home Secretary – who oversees the police, domestic security, and fighting crime – is scrutinised by the Home Affairs Select Committee.

The House of Lords

The House of Lords also scrutinises legislation, considers motions and holds debates. It has four select committees. Mostly the House of Lords agrees with the House of Commons. Frequently it proposes amendments to legislation. Sometimes it refuses to pass a Bill and sends it back to the Commons.

Once someone is a member of the House of Lords, they cannot be removed. Some support this idea – political parties have less power over them as they cannot be threatened with removal from office if they don't support a particular party. Opponents of life peers say that it allows the Government to fill the House of Lords with its own supporters.

 Discuss the importance of the House of Lords. Do you think life peers are a good thing?

Who is in the House of Lords?

In 2004, the House of Lords contained 674 members, made up of different groups who have been appointed in the following ways:

- **Hereditary peers** – 750 people who had inherited the right to be in the House of Lords from their parents. In 1999 the government passed an Act reforming the House of Lords. Now there are 92 hereditary peers.

- **Life peers** – currently 558, but the number grows each year. Life peers include 12 senior judges, known as the Law Lords. These Law Lords also sit as the highest court in the UK. There are also 24 Bishops, appointed by the Church of England.

Voting and elections

You and your vote – elections

Elections are held to choose people to represent us – in the House of Commons, the European Parliament, in regional assemblies, and on local councils. You have to be 18 or over in order to vote.

First past the post

The country is divided into 659 areas, known as constituencies. Each elects one Member of Parliament (MP) to give 659 MPs in the House of Commons.

The 'first past the post' system produces clear election results – the candidate with the most votes wins.

Proportional representation

However, the 'first past the post' system does allow a candidate to be elected on a minority of votes. For instance, one candidate may get 40% of the votes, another 35%, and another 25%. Over 60% of the voters have not supported the winning candidate – but they have not been allowed to register a preference for more than one candidate.

UK PARLIAMENT CONSITUENCY: MIDCHESTER CONSTITUENCY

VOTE FOR ONE CANDIDATE ONLY

●	**SURNAME** **Forename** Candidate's address — Party description
●	**SURNAME** **Forename** Candidate's address — Party description
●	**SURNAME** **Forename** Candidate's address — Party description
●	**SURNAME** **Forename** Candidate's address — Party description

How to vote

Your ballot paper will have all the candidates' names in alphabetical order, together with the logo of each candidate's political party. To vote, place your cross by one candidate only. Do not use numbers and don't show anyone else your ballot paper.

The alternative is proportional representation (PR) where the number of votes a party receives reflects closely the final number of seats that the party gains in the House of Commons. PR will be used in local elections in Scotland in 2007.

Critics of PR argue that it does not allow close links between a single MP and a small constituency as, instead, a group of MPs represent a larger area. Finally, PR does not produce decisive results with one party with an overall majority.

Under proportional representation, the main beneficiaries would be the Liberal Democrats, the Conservatives, and other smaller parties. The main loser would be the Labour party.

Votes at 16?

Voting age varies from country to country in the European Union. Many countries, like the UK, have a voting age of 18. However, the pressure group, Votes at 16, believes that young people of 16 should have the right to vote.

❶ What are the strongest arguments for and against votes at 16?

❷ Would you use your vote if you were 16?

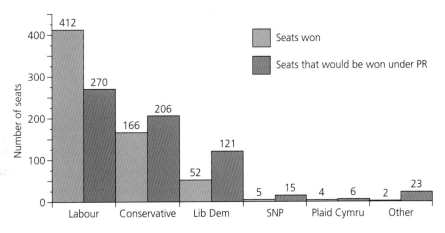

Block chart showing seats won in Great Britain in the 2001 General Election result in terms of number of seats won, and of seats that would have been won if PR had been used

FROM ELECTORAL REFORM SOCIETY

What do you think?

> "I like 'first past the post'. It's simple. You put a cross by the candidate you support, and the one with the most votes wins."
> *Tariq, Birmingham*

> "PR is more democratic – minor parties don't lose out."
> *Mel, Coventry*

> "First past the post works – one party usually gets a clear majority. And that means things actually get done."
> *Gywneth, North Wales*

 ❶ Discuss which system of election you prefer and why.

❷ Should there be a system of PR to ensure all parties are fairly represented? Or is it more important for each local area to have one dedicated MP?

Get out to vote

The idea of 'one person, one vote' has existed for men in the UK since 1884 and for women since 1928. The average turnout at a General Election has usually been between 70 and 80%. However, less than 60% voted in 2001.

Some people don't vote because they forget, or to make a political statement. Many people simply do not care, or feel that their vote does not make a difference. This is known as 'voter apathy'.

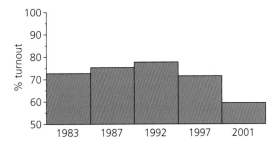

Block graph showing voting turnout in the last five General Elections in the UK

Is it worth voting?

❶ Is voter apathy a serious problem? Why do you think it is on the increase?

❷ What do you learn from the statements (right) about why vote or choose not to vote?

❸ Would you vote in a General Election, a local council or European election? Give reasons for your views.

> "I used to vote, but I gave up at the 2001 General Election. The main parties are just the same, so what's the point?"
> *Michael, Kent*

> "I always vote. People died to protect our right to vote. I respect that."
> *Glenda, Manchester*

> "Because of the electoral system, I don't vote. It doesn't matter – I've had the same MP for the last 20 years."
> *Toni, Newcastle*

> "I vote in the General Election because it's important. But I don't usually vote in local council elections – I don't know what's going on."
> *Angus, Glasgow*

Democracy

Democracy and the UK political system

Democracy means 'people power'. In the UK, we have representative democracy – representatives are elected to make decisions on our behalf. These representatives are the MPs that sit in the House of Commons (see page 31).

Representative democracy allows the opinions of a large number of people to be heard. It also allows speedy decision-making – it would be impossible for all 60 million people in the UK to be involved in every decision made.

However, representative democracy can create a distance between ordinary people and the politicians they elect to work on their behalf. In addition, very few independent politicians are elected. Instead, politicians form parties to achieve their aims and objectives.

> FOR YOUR FILE
>
> **Write a short summary of the main advantages and disadvantages of representative democracy.**

Different political systems

Below are four examples of other forms of government.

China – a Communist state

In China, there is only one political party, the Communist party. All others are forbidden. Views are sought at a local level, then they are passed upwards to a regional level, and finally to a national level. Supporters of this system call it 'grassroots democracy' as decisions flow upwards from a local area to the centre. Critics say this prevents freedom of speech and that it is open to corruption.

Switzerland – direct democracy

In Switzerland, the government is a loose collection of areas called 'cantons' (devolved government). Many decisions are made by the local population in referenda. This is known as direct democracy, allowing people a direct say. This system can be expensive, as holding referenda costs money and different decisions can be produced in different parts of the country.

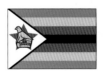

Zimbabwe – a dictatorship

A dictatorship is when one person holds absolute power – in Zimbabwe, this is President Robert Mugabe. He holds this position through illegal means: by fixing the democratic elections and by intimidating and arresting the opposition. This form of government is undemocratic, and can be violent.

Iraq – military occupation

Sometimes, the system of government breaks down and, in the case of a war, a foreign power may run the country in the absence of an elected government. Supporters of military occupation argue that it is necessary to occupy some countries to prevent them from developing weapons of mass destruction and to protect security interests. Critics say that once a war is ended, sovereignty should be transferred back to the occupied country as quickly as possible.

 Discuss each of the four systems of government. Which system do you think is the best? Which do you think is the worst? Give reasons for your views.

How the UK Government works

The Government in the UK is made up of three parts.

1. Executive
Responsible for making day-to-day decisions, such as how to spend money raised through taxation. The head of the executive is the Prime Minister.

2. Legislature
The section of Government that makes and amends laws (Parliament): the House of Commons, the House of Lords and the Monarchy (see below). The Prime Minister is head of legislature.

3. Judiciary
Made up of judges who interpret laws that the legislature has passed. Individual cases are then brought before a judge who decides whether or not the law has been broken and, if necessary, what corrective steps a person needs to take.

In the UK, the Prime Minister has wide-ranging powers as both head of the executive and head of legislature.

The Cabinet and the Opposition

The Cabinet is the main executive committee of Government made up of between 20 and 25 ministers appointed by the Prime Minister. It makes key decisions and provides leadership to the Government. The three top members of the Cabinet are:

1. **the Chancellor** – finance

2. **the Home Secretary** – law and order

3. **the Foreign Secretary** – foreign policy with other countries.

Watching the work of the Cabinet closely is the Shadow Cabinet – the main figures of the second-largest political party in the House of Commons. The head is the Leader of the Opposition. The role of the Opposition and the Shadow Cabinet is to oppose the Government and offer alternative courses of action.

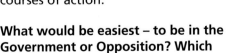 **What would be easiest – to be in the Government or Opposition? Which would be the most frustrating? Why?**

The Monarchy

In the UK, we have a monarch as our head of state. The monarch holds no real power. The current monarch is Queen Elizabeth II, who has been the head of state since 1952.

Supporters argue that is it is good to have a head of state who is non-political. Critics say that the UK should be a republic, where the head of state is elected either by politicians or the general public.

 ❶ **Do you think the monarchy is out of date?**

❷ **What would be the advantages and disadvantages of having an elected president rather than a monarch? Give reasons for your views.**

7 IT'S YOUR COUNCIL

Local government

Aim: To understand what local government is and how it functions (Citizenship 1d, 1f, 2a, 2b, 2c, 3b)

What is local government?

Local government deals with local issues. Every area in the UK has some sort of local council, made up of elected members called councillors.

The idea of local government is to elect people who have good local knowledge to make informed decisions about local issues. For example, it is better for a group of local councillors to make a decision about building a new road nearby than a civil servant in London.

Different types of local government

Local government has either one or two main levels: in Scotland, Wales, Northern Ireland, London, or in a major city, there is probably one local council responsible for all local services. These are called Unitary Authorities in some areas and Metropolitan Boroughs in others.

In the remaining areas of England, excluding most major cities, there are two main levels of local government: County Councils and District Councils.

County Councils are responsible for education, social services and local transport. Within each County Council, there are five or six smaller District Councils, responsible for planning, rubbish collection, housing and leisure facilities. District Councils often have to co-ordinate their work with their local County Council.

Local councillors – who are they and what do they do?

Local councillors are ordinary members of the public who are elected to represent a local area – or ward. Wards can elect up to three councillors, depending on what type of council they represent and how large it is.

Local councillors have a number of duties:
- attending council meetings every four to six weeks, to debate and make decisions.
- representing the council at meetings of the local fire or police authorities.
- trying to solve the problems of local people (casework).

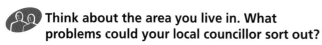 **Think about the area you live in. What problems could your local councillor sort out?**

Getting involved – surgeries, questions and deputations

1 Most councillors hold regular surgeries (drop-in sessions) to listen to local residents' problems.

2 Many local councils allow members of the public to ask questions or make short speeches (deputations) at council meetings. This could be to ask what the council is doing to sort out a particular problem, or to make a speech arguing why a problem needs solving.

 ❶ **What three questions would you like to ask your local council? Why?**

❷ **Compare your questions with that of other pairs.**

Standing to be a local councillor

In order to stand as a local councillor, you have to:

- be over 21 years of age
- have a local connection to the area.

However, you cannot become a councillor if you have been made bankrupt in the last five years, as you will be making decisions about public money!

Local councillors receive an allowance to compensate for the time they must take off work. They can also claim expenses for travelling to meetings. And councillors are entitled by law to take time off work in order to fulfil their duties.

Mark Coles, 21, is a local Lib Dem councillor for Ceredigion, Wales

In order to encourage applications from a variety of people, the Government has suggested reducing the number of councillors, but offer the remaining councillors a full-time salary for a full-time job.

 Should local councillors be full-time? Or is it better to have part-time councillors who can bring experience from other areas? Give reasons for your views.

Case study: Planning decisions

One of the powers councils have is the power to make planning decisions. If anyone wants to build a new road, extend their house, change a shop into several small flats, or make any other major change to their property, they must first get the permission of the council's planning department.

If the planning application conforms with the local plan, the application will be accepted. If it is rejected, the person making the application can appeal to the government. This is done through the office of the Deputy Prime Minister.

 ❶ Are there any planning decisions you would like to see made in your local area?

❷ Are there any past decisions (for example, the building of a controversial road or flats) that you disagree with? Give reasons for your views.

Planning applications

Sometimes, the local council will demand money from a developer, in return for allowing a planning application.

 Imagine that a developer wants to build 100 new flats in your local area. Decide which of the following you will demand in return for planning permission.

- A new playground for children who will move into the flats.
- A new road so the flats can be easily accessed.
- Landscaping to hide the flats from view for the local residents.

Give reasons for your decision.

Local government

Aim: To examine how local government could be reformed in order to reduce the democratic deficit that exists in UK politics (Citizenship 1d, 1f, 2a, 2b, 2c, 3b)

What is the democratic deficit?

One of the key functions of a democracy is to involve the people. However, in local government the number of people voting has fallen to 25%. This has created a gap between the government and people who do not vote – the democratic deficit. Some people feel that local government does not solve the problems they are interested in. As a result they become indifferent to politics leading to voter apathy. One idea is to change the voting system (see page 33).

In recent years, the Government has changed the structure of local councils to try to make them more democratic.

Changing the structure within local government

Directly elected mayors

In 2002, local councils were given the power to hold a referendum so people could decide whether to directly elect a mayor. The mayor would then be responsible for all decisions, scrutinised by local councillors.

Some cities voted in favour of directly elected mayors. Supporters argue it leads to quick decision-making for which one individual is responsible. Critics of the system argue it gives one person too much power.

Local cabinets and scrutiny panels

Another alternative is for councillors to elect a cabinet of between seven and nine councillors to make decisions. Individual areas, such as housing, transport or the environment, has its own cabinet member. Some decisions are made by individual cabinet members, others by the cabinet as a whole.

All the decisions are scrutinised by ordinary council members, or scrutiny panels. Final decisions are then also approved by all councillors.

Supporters argue that this system is democratic as it involves all councils, but critics say that if one party gets a majority on the council, it can control the scrutiny panels and strongly affect decisions made.

The Mayor of London, Ken Livingstone, who was the driving force in introducing the congestion charge in Central London

> "I like the idea of directly elected mayors. Having one person responsible for local government in each council is a good idea."
> **Douglas, Watford**

> "We elect councillors so they should all be involved in as much decision-making as possible."
> **Katherine, Oxford**

> "Local councils don't make a difference – it's the Houses of Parliament that really matter."
> **Tony, Plymouth**

 Discuss the views above and say why you agree or disagree with them.

Involving local people

Residents associations

In some areas, such as parts of Birmingham and London, local residents would like more influence over decisions. They have set up local resident associations to voice their views.

Neighbourhood management

Neighbourhood management is part of the local council, with the power to make decisions and control small budgets. Each area would hold regular elections to elect an Executive Committee.

Neighbourhood management also includes local people who represent the views of residents in one particular street. They report any problems in the area to the local council.

Local referenda

Another possibility is to hold local referenda where, on controversial decisions, there could be a vote held by all the residents.

Referenda where votes are taken at polling stations are expensive to organise. However, votes could be made by post or the internet. This would be an example of direct democracy – decisions being made by local people, for local people.

Critics of local referenda ask why would people bother electing local councillors? They also argue that small scale local referenda through the post and the internet would be open to fraud and abuse.

Midchester internet ballot

Please vote for your preferred candidate by clicking his/her name.

○ Mary Birt (Conservative)
○ Nana Gremah (Labour)
○ David Sneesby (Lib Dem)
○ Tony Morrison (Green)
○ Shirin Smith (Independent)

[Cast my vote]

 Look at the three different ways of involving local people in local decisions above. Which do you think works best? Give reasons for your views.

Involving young people

Pressure groups, such as the British Youth Council, say there is a particular democratic deficit amongst young people – election turnout is lower for under-25s, and only over-18s can vote.

One solution has been to set up a Youth Parliament. Young people, aged 14–18, gather together to discuss local politics. Then they elect one person to be the member of the Youth Parliament for their local area.

Another idea has been to create a local Youth Council – young people who meet to discuss local problems.

 ❶ **How could more young people be involved in local decision-making in your area? Write a list of action points.**

❷ **Compare your ideas with other groups.**

Local government

Aim: To understand what devolution is and how it is changing UK politics – nationally and locally
(Citizenship 1d, 1f, 2a, 2b, 2c, 3b)

What is devolution?

Devolution means the transfer of power from one central point to many smaller, different areas. At a national level, this means the UK Parliament transferring power from Westminster to the Scottish Parliament, or to the London, Welsh or Northern Ireland Assembly. At a local level, this means councils transferring some of their powers to community cabinets (see right) or neighbourhood management (see page 39).

Where is there devolution nationally?

Devolution was introduced in Northern Ireland in 1998, in Scotland and Wales in 1999, and in London in 2000. Before devolution was introduced, a referendum was held in each area to decide whether or not the local population was in favour.

In Autumn 2004, the North-East of England held a referendum to decide whether some power would be transferred from the UK Parliament at Westminster to a new regional assembly to be based in Newcastle. A majority voted against the proposed assembly.

Opponents of devolution argue that devolution undermines the authority of the UK Parliament at Westminster. Supporters of devolution argue that having different solutions for different areas is precisely the point of devolution.

 Look at the map. Is there devolution in your area? If so, can you name any changes devolution has made locally? If not, do you think devolution for your area is a good idea? Give reasons for your views.

Red shaded areas are where devolution has been introduced in the UK. Blue shaded areas are where devolution is being considered

Case study: Devolution at work in the Scottish Parliament

The Scottish Parliament held its first elections in 1999, using a form of proportional representation. It has 129 members, or Members of the Scottish Parliament (MSPs). In 2004 the Scottish Parliament was run by a coalition of the Labour Party and the Liberal Democrats.

For the majority of major decisions, the Scottish Parliament has worked well. Major decisions include abolishing the student loan system in Scotland, banning hunting, and introducing free care for the elderly in nursing homes. However, in at least one area there have been problems. In order to house the Scottish Parliament, a new building was built at Holyrood. The costs of constructing this new building have soared – expenditure that was meant to be controlled by the Scottish Parliament.

Does devolution really matter?

Opponents naturally say no and point to low turnouts at elections for devolved governments. Supporters say yes, as it is another opportunity for decisions to be taken which reflect the views of a particular area. Perhaps more important is what actual practical decisions are made that affect people's day-to-day lives.

By contrast, the Scottish and Welsh National Parties believe there should be an independent Scotland and Wales, with their own Parliaments. These would then be separate countries, independent of the UK, within the European Union. Thus, both of these parties are demanding a referendum in their area to decide whether Scotland or Wales should become independent.

What do you think?

> "Devolution is a waste of money – why can't all the decisions be made at Westminster. We don't need any more assemblies."
>
> *Jill, Norfolk*

> "Devolution is great, but it's just a stepping stone for full independence for Wales."
>
> *Gwyneth, Conwy*

> "I support devolution. But that's far enough, there shouldn't be an independent Scotland or Wales."
>
> *Angus, Aberdeen*

 Discuss these views and say why you agree or disagree with them.

Local devolution and community cabinets

Local devolution is about councils giving more power to local areas inside the council. One way of doing this is for the council to transfer responsibility for its budgets to a lower area. This can be done in the case of neighbourhood management (see page 39). Alternatively, community cabinets can be set up.

A community cabinet is made up of only those councillors that represent a small area within the council. These councillors can then set different priorities in the budgets they control for their particular area.

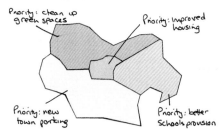

Midchester Town Plan

Community cabinets allow money to be spent on schemes specific to an area

 Do you think community cabinets are a good idea? Where do you think there could be a community cabinet for your area?

Case study: Going local in Birmingham

Birmingham Council represents over 10 parliamentary constituencies and over 500,000 people. The council is made up of over 120 councillors. Each councillor represents a ward with two other councillors, and each ward has around 14,000 people in it.

In 2001, Birmingham Council held a consultation exercise and decided that for many decisions the council was too big and unwieldy. In addition, each of 11 distinct communities had different priorities and wanted money spending on different areas.

As a result, Birmingham decided to launch the 'Going Local' project. Many council powers were devolved to community cabinets, known as district committees. In the first phase, control over leisure centres, swimming pools, libraries, doorstep recycling and refuse collection, street cleaning, grounds maintenance, parks management, community development, arts and play areas, and management of car parks, have all be transferred from the council to district committees.

8 WORKING FOR CHANGE

How can you change things?

Aim: To discuss pressure groups and campaigning in your town or local area
(Citizenship 1f, 2a, 2b, 2c, 3b, 3c)

What are pressure groups?

Political pressure is when you try and influence somebody to make a decision. For example, in your local area, a number of people may try to persuade a council not to build houses on an environmental site. These people may form an organisation to influence decision-makers. This is known as a pressure group.

Single-issue pressure groups

There are many different types of pressure group. Some groups may only campaign on particular issues. These are known as single-issue pressure groups. Examples include London 2012, whose single issue is to bring the Olympics to London in 2012.

Case study: The Hastings by-pass

Many single-issue pressure groups exist only for a limited amount of time. For example, in 2004, the Government proposed building a by-pass around the town of Hastings in East Sussex. The by-pass was controversial in that it crossed several important environmental sites – known as sites of special scientific interest. However, those in favour of the by-pass argued that it would help relieve traffic congestion in the town, with a positive effect of reducing traffic pollution in Hastings.

Sectional pressure groups

There are also pressure groups that campaign on a wide range of interests. These are known as sectional pressure groups. For example:

- *Civic Societies*, which campaign to protect local architecture
- *Neighbourhood Watch*, which exists to help the police and fight crime in the local area
- *Residents Associations*, which aim to represent the views of local residents.

❶ Can you think of any pressure groups that exist in your local area? How long have they existed?

❷ Do you think these groups will still be campaigning in your area in 10 years time?

Setting up a pressure group

If you decided to set up a pressure group in your area, there are several steps that you need to follow:

1. Choose the issue or area that you want to campaign for.

2. Check that are no other pressure groups already concentrating on the issue you want to campaign on.

3. Decide on a specific aim for your pressure group. For example: single-issue group: to stop the Bloggs housing development from being built on Nicetown's Green Belt; sectional pressure group: to promote the interests of young people in Smallville.

4. Choose a name for your pressure group. This should be something catchy and memorable, and should be relevant to the aims of your group.

5. Decide who makes decisions that will affect your pressure group, and then target them. This could be the local council, your local MP or local companies.

6. Decide who you need to support your pressure group. This may include those people targeted in the previous box, along with members of the general public and the local media.

7. Decide how you will raise money for your pressure group.

8. Decide how you will try to gain public support.

9. Decide how you will get in contact with other groups that share your aims and ambitions.

10. Decide how you will measure the success of your pressure group.

 Imagine you have to set up your own pressure group. Follow the steps in the flowchart, and then compare your ideas with other groups in your class.

Getting things done

In order to influence decision-makers, pressure groups use a variety of methods to persuade people to support their point of view and to get their message across, such as:

- writing press releases and letters to the press
- organising a stall at a local market or town square
- running a petition, asking people to support a particular issue
- holding public meetings
- asking people to donate money, or join their pressure group as a member
- organising publicity stunts, including marches and public protests.

 Which of the above methods do you think are the most effective? Why?

National pressure groups

Aim: To discuss what pressure groups exist nationally and how they campaign
(Citizenship 1f, 2a, 2b, 2c, 3b, 3c)

What pressure groups are there?

Many pressure groups campaign on issues that affect people on a national and, sometimes, an international level. As a result, there are several differences between local and national pressure groups.

A More pressure groups exist on a national level. This is because the number of people interested in a national issue is greater, so there are more opportunities for national pressure groups to be created.

B There tend to be more sectional pressure groups (see page 42) than specific interest groups on a national level. Well-known examples are the Royal Society for the Prevention of Cruelty to Animals (RSPCA) and the Countryside Alliance.

C National campaigns can be larger and more hard-hitting. Examples include Action for Smoking Health (ASH), which is campaigning to ban smoking in public places.

D National pressure groups tend to last longer. Because the issues are larger, it takes more time to resolve them. One example is the Campaign for Nuclear Disarmament (www.cnduk.org) which was set up in 1958 and is still campaigning against nuclear armament.

1 Think about which national pressure groups have been in the news recently. Discuss how they have been successful in getting their message across.

2 Are you, your parents or your friends members of a national pressure group? Discuss the reasons for joining.

Trade Unions

Another type of national pressure group are Trade Unions. These are made up of groups of workers who form a pressure group to protect their own interests. The right to form a Trade Union is recognised in a variety of human rights legislation.

Trade Unions are a major force in British politics. Some Trade Unions have close links with the Labour Party. The majority of Trade Unions have merged to form a super-sized pressure group – the Trades Union Congress (TUC). This exists to protect the interests of all Trade Unions and their members who belong to the TUC in the UK.

Trade Unions have special legal rights under the law in the UK. This includes the right to be consulted about changes in the working conditions of their members. Trade Unions also use different campaign techniques to ordinary pressure groups, such as strike action. This is where members of a Trade Union refuse to work until their demands are met. This is often seen as a last resort by the Trade Unions.

Working to rule means that members of a Trade Union will only do the minimum of their working duties set out in their job description.

> "Trade Unions are a great idea – every workplace should have a Trade Union."
> *Arthur, Doncaster*

> "Trade Unions give workers too much power – it is employers that should be running companies."
> *Margaret, London*

> "Negotiating is one thing, but strike action is another. Unions should be allowed, but strikes should be banned."
> *Donald, Lincoln*

 Discuss which of the above statements you agree with. Give reasons for your views.

The National Union of Students exists to promote student's interests in higher education. Imagine you had to set up a Students' Union at your school. What local and national issues would you want to campaign on? Why?

Students protesting against university fees

Lobbying

Lobbying is a technique that pressure groups use to influence key decisions. It involves trying to persuade the decision-maker to accept a particular point of view. The phrase 'lobby' comes from the area known as the central lobby in the Houses of Parliament, where people come to meet their MP to try to influence them.

Pressure groups may employ staff to lobby decision-makers, such as MPs and Ministers, or employ specialists (lobbyists) to lobby on their behalf.

Some people think lobbyists are helpful, as they allow government to make informed decisions by providing them with extra information. Other people think they get in the way, as the person with the most money can hire the best lobbyists.

Pressure groups or political parties?

In the UK, there is increasing dissatisfaction with political parties, and this is reflected in the declining turnout in elections (see page 32). However, the membership of pressure groups keep on growing. For example, the Royal Society for the Protection of Birds (RSPB) has more members than the three largest political parties in the UK combined.

This has led to some people believing the pressure groups are more effective than political parties. Supporters of pressure groups say that this is positive, arguing that pressure groups help to fill the democratic deficit. Critics argue that this is dangerous because pressure groups can hijack the political agenda and not see the 'big' picture.

 Which are you more likely to join – a pressure group or a political party? Give reasons for your views.

9 DEVELOPING YOUR IDENTITY AND IMAGE

A sense of identity

Aim: To explore your sense of identity, and your feelings about image and becoming an adult
(PSHE 1a, 1b, 1c, 1d)

Who are we?

What kind of adult?

Adolescence is all about changing from a child into an adult. But, Janet Lake asks, what kind of adult do you want to be?

Yes, adults are crazy, annoying, embarrassing, OLD... but you're turning into one, remember? (Some of you may even feel you've got there already.) Becoming an adult is the main point of adolescence, so it's worth spending some time thinking about the kind of adult you want to be. What qualities do you want to have? What skills and abilities? What characteristics do you definitely *not* want to have?

Draw up a table like the one below. (The qualities listed are only an example – everyone will feel differently about this...)
It may help to think about adults that you respect, especially those of the same sex, whether they are members of your family or public figures. And, of course, adults you don't want to turn into...

HOW I WANT TO BE AS AN ADULT	HOW I DON'T WANT TO BE AS AN ADULT
Coping	Indecisive
Strong	Nagging
Dynamic	Stressed

Remember, there is no right or wrong answer to the question "What kind of adult do you want to be?". But the qualities you jot down will tell you a lot about your emerging identity.

❶ **On your own, draw up a list of qualities, as Janet Lake describes.**

❷ **Share your list with your partner and explain why you have included these qualities in your list. How similar or different are your lists?**

❸ **Discuss whether you think your lists will change in the next five to 10 years. If so, how?**

❹ **What do you think your lists say about your 'emerging identity'?**

Beckham trounces Jesus in poll to find youth heroes

Jesus scored only a handful of votes – the same number as US President George W Bush – in a survey of young Britons' heroes. They both came 123rd – near the bottom of a list topped by soccer celebrity David Beckham (first), Hollywood heart-throb Brad Pitt (second) and pop star Justin Timberlake (third).

Prime Minister Tony Blair shared 69th place with master illusionist David Blaine.

Psychologists asked more than 2,500 young people, aged between 16 and 24, to nominate the individuals they most admired.

Study leader Dr Adrian North, from the University of Leicester, said: "Although people could have voted for great political thinkers or artists, their top 10 comprised Hollywood stars, pop musicians and a footballer. They went for people with nothing much to say but who look good. It's slightly depressing really. What links all the names in our top ten is not their great minds but their great looks."

He thought this was not particularly surprising when young people were continually bombarded with powerful media images that emphasise beauty and youth.

FROM *THE DAILY MAIL*

❶ **Do you agree with Dr North that the findings of his poll are 'depressing'?**

❷ **Share who your top three heroes would have been. What qualities do they have that makes them heroes?**

DESIGNER CLOTHES

Designer Wayne Hemingway lets us know what he thinks of that scourge of every parent – the 'must have' designer clothes labels demanded by many of our kids

Why r so many kids dressed in the identikit uniform of Nike/Adidas/Reebok et al? Parents argue that the kids demand it – well how weak spirited + old fashioned of u! Explain to them that: 1. Its old fashioned to wear logos 2. Its cooler to be an individual than look the same as everyone else + that individuals r the ones that go on + make money. 3. It's a waste of money! 4. Its daft to pay to be a walking billboard – shouldn't it be the other way round?

FROM WWW.FATHERSDIRECT.COM

What do you think?

> "There is a lot of pressure on teenagers to appear cool. That means wearing the right brands. Like it or not, that's the way it is."
>
> *Damian*

❶ **Read the article on designer clothes and the quote below it. Do you agree with Wayne Hemingway that 'it's cooler to be an individual than look the same as everyone else'? Or do you agree with Damian that it's cool to wear the right brands?**

❷ **Discuss your attitudes to clothes and why you dress the way you do.**

Write a statement under the heading 'Who am I?' to describe your own identity. Think about the following aspects of your identity and write one paragraph on each:

- **Your personality** – the features of your character that make you the person you are
- **Your appearance,** including your clothes, and your attitude to your appearance
- **Your goals and ambitions** – what kind of adult you want to be, and what you hope to achieve in the next 10 years.

Influences on behaviour and self-image

Who influences your behaviour?

The gay rapper

He's white, he's English, he's homosexual. Can QBoy possibly fit into the notoriously bigoted world of hip-hop?

Marcos Brito can't be expecting his career to run smoothly. A 25-year-old from Basildon, Essex, he is also the UK's first openly homosexual hip-hopper. And, as QBoy, he has no plans to let homophobia stand in his way. "For so long I limited myself by telling myself I couldn't be a rapper because I'm white, English and gay," he says. "Now I've become a rapper, it's made me realise you only limit yourself – no one else limits you."

FROM AN ARTICLE BY HATTIE COLLINS, *THE GUARDIAN*

The importance of parents

When we are children we believe our parents are God-like – 'all-powerful' beings who are in control of it all. We naturally trust them and believe everything they say, and this trust makes us feel secure.

Then, at some point, most of us have this illusion shattered and we realise that our parents aren't actually perfect. From that point on, we lose some of our childhood innocence and start to look at things – and adults – differently.

It can be a painful awakening. But, although painful, this process can also empower us to be more in command of our lives. We can finally figure out who we are and make decisions for ourselves, rather than just echoing our parents' choices and identities.

FROM *SISTERS UNLIMITED* BY JESSICA HOWIE

 **1** Discuss what influences you think QBoy has had to battle with to succeed.

2 How powerful a role are prejudices and stereotypes in influencing you and your behaviour?

3 Do you agree with Jessica Howie that parents lose their influence on you some time during your adolescence?

4 How important is it for your self-development that you break away from your parents' influence?

 On your own, make a list of all the different influences on your behaviour, such as family, friends, role models, media, religion, teachers. Rank them in order and share your list with your partner.

Give a teen a bad name: labels

Listen to what family members say about each other. Consider the nicknames, the stories told about each other and the jokes. These are the signs that family members are cast into roles and given labels to match.

"Oh, he's the clever one in the family but he's got no common sense."

"She's a bit of a tearaway."

"My youngest is such a scaredy cat, she's nervous about absolutely everything!"

Labelling is disabling

Although it may be true that your child is more fearful than other children, labelling him as 'fearful' may make things worse. Labels – good or bad – become a part of the child's self image. Although a label may start with a germ of truth in it, it quickly acquires its own force. A 'clumsy' child becomes apprehensive about picking up something delicate and in a state of nervousness, drops it. More proof that he is clumsy!

Sulky...

Kind...

Thoughtful...

Moody...

Considerate...

Selfish...

Good labels, bad labels and labels in pairs

Parents often label their children by comparing and contrasting them. First children are often 'nervous and shy' and their younger siblings 'outgoing and sociable'. Some labels link the child to another member of the family – 'You're just like your father'.

Even good can be bad

Positive as well as negative labels have their downside. A child constantly labelled as the 'responsible one' in the family, feels he always has to be on his best behaviour. His 'real self' is both responsible and reckless. Sometimes he feels the desire to break out and be irresponsible but the label inhibits him. He may also fear that his parents only like the responsible boy and if they see the 'real boy' they won't like it or him.

WWW.RAISINGKIDS.CO.UK

 1 Discuss what you have found out about labelling. How can good labels be bad?

2 Think of some labels that you apply to yourself. Where have they come from? What are they really based on?

3 Challenge your labels and help your partner challenge theirs.

Challenge your labels

"If you have labels on yourself, like 'I am a slow learner', 'I am uncoordinated', 'I can't multiply', ask yourself, 'What's the proof?' Challenge your labels. When we give ourselves a second chance, and get some help, most often we can do it."

Andrew Matthews

FROM *BEING A HAPPY TEENAGER* BY ANDREW MATTHEWS (Seashell Publishers, Australia)

10 MANAGING YOUR EMOTIONS & MOODS

How do you manage how you feel?

Aim: To explore how to manage difficult moods and emotions, focusing on anger and disappointment (PSHE 1a, 1b, 1c, 1d, 3e, 3f)

What is anger?

We all feel angry sometimes. Some people tend to become angry easily (a 'short fuse'), and some have problems controlling their anger. Anger has consequences, such as hurting other people – more usually their feelings, but sometimes physically. The after-effects of anger often make a person feel guilty and ashamed, but anger is a normal emotion.

Anger generally results from our feeling helpless or unable to control certain situations. We feel as if we are trapped by circumstances and can't see any way out.

Expressing and controlling anger

The instinctive, natural way to express anger is to respond aggressively. Anger is a natural reaction to threats; it allows us to fight and to defend ourselves when we are attacked. We need a certain amount of anger to survive. On the other hand, we can't physically lash out at every person or object that annoys us.

Here are some ways to deal with angry feelings.

1 **Express your angry feelings assertively**, not aggressively. To do this, you have to learn how to make clear what your needs are – and how to get them met – without hurting others. Being assertive doesn't mean being pushy or demanding; it means being respectful of yourself and others.

2 **Suppress anger**, and then redirect it by holding in your anger, stop thinking about it and focus on something positive. Physical exercise is very effective, as is redirecting your feelings into a hobby or an interest.

3 **Calm down!** This means not just controlling how you act, but learning to relax.

4 **Find out** what is causing you to feel angry – and then find ways of dealing with that. Talk to others who are involved and try to find ways of removing that trigger.

5 **Avoid alcohol** – If you drink you will have less control over your actions. Alcohol is most often the fuel behind violence.

> ### ANGER FIRST AID
>
> - Walk away! Come back later.
> - Try to 'count to 10' slowly.
> - Take deep and slow breaths, concentrating as you breathe.
> - Go out for a run, walk or bike ride.
> - If all else fails – thump a cushion or kick a bean bag. (DON'T do anything that will hurt yourself or someone else.)
> - When you feel calmer, talk to those you were with at the time and explain why you were feeling that way – calmly!

FROM WWW.CWGSY.NET/COMMUNITY/MINDINFO/ANGER.HTM

① Discuss what makes you angry and how you deal with your anger.

② Which are the best tips in the article for dealing with anger?

③ When do you think you need to apply 'anger first aid'?

HOW DO YOU DEAL WITH DISAPPOINTMENTS?

You apply for a part-time job and your friend gets hired. Maybe you get a new car and it gets stolen within a week. Or you fall in love with the guy next door and he falls in love with the girl across the street.

When these things happen, you have a few options. You can either:

- Ask yourself, **"Why do bad things always happen to me?"** This gets you stranded in self-pity, an option for losers. While we feel sorry for ourselves, we never do anything to fix a problem.

- Tell yourself, **"It's not my fault."** This is another excuse to do nothing. Even if it's not your fault, the question is, "What are you going to do about it?".

- Ask yourself, **"What do I learn from this?"** This is how you bounce back. You ask yourself, what do I learn, what else can I do, who can help me? Then you make a plan to deal with disappointment.

If you believe (or even pretend) that every event in your life has a purpose, you will learn from your disappointments. We are not here to be punished. We are here to be educated.

> In a nutshell:
> You are never beaten until you quit!

It's OK to be wrong

Let's say you try out for the lead in the school play, and you discover you don't like acting. That's terrific. You've discovered something more about yourself. Tick it off the list. Now you can say, "Forget Hollywood!" How else would you know but by trying?

Imagine you begin a law degree and don't like it. That's OK. (I know – I started law and hated it!) How else could you know but by trying?

You become happy and prosperous by doing lots of things, making plenty of mistakes, and taking the time to learn from things that didn't work.

> In a nutshell:
> Failure is not an end; failure is a beginning. The question is, "Does failure make you bitter, or does it make you better?"

FROM *BEING A HAPPY TEENAGER* BY ANDREW MATTHEWS (Seashell Publishers, Australia)

① Read about dealing with disappointments and failure, and discuss whether you agree with the author's views and advice.

② Think of a 'failure' or 'disappointment' that you have suffered and tell your partner how it affected you. Did it make you bitter, or did it make you better? How could you have dealt with it differently, and what effect might that have had?

Assertiveness

Aim: To explore what assertiveness is, and how to be assertive (PSHE 1a, 1b, 1c, 1d, 3e, 3f)

How to be assertive without being aggressive *by Caro Handley*

Think of someone who has a seemingly natural air of authority, who gets things done and is listened to without ever shouting, threatening, bribing, sulking or crying. There aren't many of them around, but assertive people stand out a mile when you come across them.

In contrast, there are plenty of aggressive people around who use bullying tactics and think they're being assertive. To be assertive is to be neither a doormat nor a bully. And what's more, it's possible for anyone to learn how to do it, with a bit of effort and patience.

Don't dilute

Don't be wishy-washy about what you are saying or asking for. Too often people apologise, make excuses or give long explanations so that the person listening is given a very mixed message. Never say things like: "I'm sorry to have to ask you this...", "I feel awful about this, but..." or "I wouldn't ask, only..."

Be clear and direct

Work out in advance what it is you want to say and then say it as clearly and directly as you can, with no extra frills. Sound as though you know what you want or what you think, and people will believe you and know where they stand with you.

Use few words

The fewer words you use, the bigger the impact. Powerful, effective people are always succinct. Try to listen more often than you speak.

Be positive

Make sure that you are friendly and warm without being slimy or toadying – smile when you ask someone to do something and always thank them afterwards.

Pay attention

People will take you far more seriously if you look directly at them and give the conversation your full attention. A hasty order barked over your shoulder or muttered while doing something else will make the other person feel as though they don't matter, and may also give the impression that you don't mean what you say.

ADAPTED FROM WWW.IVILLAGE.CO.UK/WORKCAREER/SURVIVE/

1 Read the article on assertiveness and discuss what you have learned.

2 What is the difference between assertiveness and aggression?

3 How assertive do you think you are, and how could you improve your assertiveness?

FOR YOUR FILE

Practise your assertiveness skills using one of the following situations:
- Your brother or sister has borrowed something without asking
- You lent your friend a CD and it comes back scratched
- Your parent lays into you for leaving the kitchen in a mess (it was really your sister).

Write about how you deal with the situation aggressively, and then how you deal with the same situation in an assertive way.

A quarrel a day...

... keeps the doctor away, says Anne Nicholls. An argument can be good for your health, as it is better to stand up for yourself than to bottle up your anger. But there are good and bad ways to argue. Here are some tips:

1 Bawling at your boyfriend

17-year-old Karen is queen when it comes to arguing with her boyfriend, Lewis. "It'll annoy me sometimes if he's been chatting to other girls or spending too much time glued to his PlayStation. He doesn't seem to notice I'm upset, so I'll have to pick a fight to let him know what's been bugging me."

FIGHT FACTOR Anne says: "During a row, avoid the 'And another thing...' trap. After all, if he keeps doing something you object to, why not just try to accept your differences and move on? However, if arguing does resolve things, it can only be positive."

2 Friendly fallout

Sometimes even our best friends can bug the hell out of us. 18-year-old Chrissie was having problems: "My friend Anna can be really thoughtless at times, cancelling our plans last minute."

FIGHT FACTOR "Give her specific examples of times she's upset you," advises Anne. "Sometimes people don't actually realise they've upset you." Chrissie tried this: "After Anna cancelled our plans again I told her she was being insensitive and detailed each time she'd let me down. She realised how inconsiderate she'd been and now we both make more of an effort."

3 Punch-up with parents

Rowing with our parents is far too easily done, but there is a risk of rowing with them almost out of habit. "I realised I was acting like a stroppy madam around my parents, particularly when it came to things like what time I'd be home at night," says Jade, 17. "The thing is, I know that, unlike a friend or boyfriend, I can say almost anything in an argument with my parents without worrying about losing them."

FIGHT FACTOR Anne advises: "Let your parents know that you value their love and care for you and they're more likely to consider your needs. Helping out at home, making them cups of tea, and chatting about their interests as well as yours, shows them you are mature and will invite their trust."

ADAPTED FROM *19*

1 Discuss arguments. How exactly can arguing be good for your health?

2 Analyse the three case studies in 'A quarrel a day' and jot down factors that make the argument unsuccessful and unhealthy. What factors make it successful and healthy?

FOR YOUR FILE

Write a piece for a teenage advice website on 'How to have a good argument'.

11 THINKING AHEAD – planning your future

Assessing your skills and investigating careers

Aim: To begin thinking about careers, based on an assessment of your personal skills (PSHE 1f, 1g)

Which career?

Hundreds of careers and only one lifetime – how on earth do you decide what's best for you? Maybe you're one of the lucky ones: you know what you want, and you know exactly what's needed to get there.

Don't worry if you're unsure or a bit confused about all the choices. Probably half the population already working would say they're equally unsure or confused about what they want to do when they 'grow up'!

Nowadays many people totally change career directions two, three, or even more, times in their life. So if you do start off in the 'wrong' job, there's nothing to stop you changing later on. If you're flexible and willing to re-train where necessary, you're laughing!

FROM WWW.PROSPECTS.CO.UK/CAREERS/

Start with yourself

Knowing more about yourself will help you choose a career that suits you. Follow these steps:

1 Write down:
- something your best friend likes about you
- something about you that your best friend wants you to improve
- something your parents/carers say is good about you
- something your parents/carers criticise about you
- something good that your tutor has written or said is good about you
- something your tutor is always asking you to improve.

2 Then write down:
- your best quality
- something you think you need to improve
- a recent achievement which you are proud of
- something you wish you'd done better.

3 Discuss what you have written with a partner. Adjust as necessary.

4 Finally, write a statement about yourself that describes your strengths and the areas for improvement. Can you suggest some careers that may suit someone with your strengths and weaknesses?

FROM STEP THREE 2003–4

Skills 4 Jobs

Skills can be divided into five main areas:

1. People skills:
- communication
- inspiration
- negotiation
- delegation
- advising

2. Thinking skills:
- evaluating
- problem solving
- proritising
- weighing up evidence and alternatives

3. Using information:
- memorising
- researching
- calculating
- organising
- observing

4. Helping people get things done:
- coordinating and liaising
- overseeing
- planning
- recognising other people's talents and skills

5. Seeing things from a different angle
- finding alternatives
- thinking laterally
- flair and imagination
- seeing potential
- finding links

ADAPTED FROM *YOUR FUTURE*

Job families

There are so many jobs available that sometimes it is easier to break them down into job families. The table below lists some job families and what they involve.

SCIENTIFIC

finding out why and how things work, applying science

SOCIAL SERVICE

helping people with problems, caring for them

LITERARY

using the written or spoken word

ARTISTIC

applying a creative skill in art, design, music or drama

GENERAL SERVICE

providing a service to the public

MECHANICAL

making, using or repairing machinery

NATURAL

working with plants, animals and other natural resources

NUMERICAL

working with figures or solving mathematical problems

PRACTICAL

being directly involved in making products

DRIVING

driving a vehicle

OUTDOOR/ACTIVE

being out and about, and physically active

FROM *OPTIONS AT 16+*,
A CONNEXIONS GLOUCESTERSHIRE PUBLICATION

① Look at the list of skills in the article 'Skills 4 Jobs'. Discuss what skills you think you have. Choose four or five skills from the list.

② Now look at the list of job families. What kinds of job would make the best use of your skills?

③ Find some job adverts in local or national newspapers. Which jobs would you be most interested in? Do you feel your skills fit these jobs best?

FOR YOUR FILE

Choose a career that interests you. Use the internet, careers library, or talk to people already doing this job. Write a report, including what activities you would do, where and who you would work with, how much you would earn, and what skills and qualifications you need

Why work experience?

Preparing for work experience

Some time during Year 10 you will go on a work experience placement. The activities on this spread are designed to prepare you for this and to help you get the most out of it.

Why bother with work experience?

Don't let the words 'work experience' fill you with fear. It's a way of exploring the world of work – from the inside. And, whether it is in a factory or a hospital, a work placement could help you to get a job when you leave school.

Taking part in a work placement will benefit you in a variety of ways:

- It will help you to decide if your dream job really is a dream or is, in fact, a nightmare.
- You will learn what it is really like going to work every day and doing a job.
- Your team-working, time-keeping and communication skills will all benefit.
- You will practise using your initiative (and asking for help, should you need it).
- You may even end up with a job, if you work hard and impress your boss.

Case study: Jas – in the shadows

Jas has always wanted to be a solicitor, so she was pleased that she was going to a solicitor's on work experience. On her placement she visited the law courts and the local police station. However, most of her time was spent in the office where she researched information and carried out clerical work, like photocopying. She also shadowed (followed) a solicitor, who spent most of his time reading, writing letters and talking to clients on the telephone. She felt law was not as glamorous as she had thought – there was too much paperwork!

Case study: Mark – a cut above

Mark does not know what he wants to do when he leaves school. Teachers think he is shy, lacking confidence, and not always reliable. He didn't care where he went for work experience. The only placement left was at the local hairdresser. Mark had to talk to customers, wash their hair, sweep the floor, make cups of tea, and take telephone bookings. He turned up on time every day and enjoyed chatting to customers in the shop and on the phone. The hairdressers were very impressed with him and have offered him a part-time job in the school holidays.

FROM JACKIE REYNOLDS

 ❶ Discuss the reasons you have for doing work experience.

❷ What particular skills – either personal or practical – do you want to practise or develop?

❸ From the two case studies, what do you think Jas and Mark learned from their work experience?

FOR YOUR FILE

When you have chosen a placement and completed an application form, you will need to send a covering letter. Write a paragraph on:
- why you think work experience is important,
- what you can offer the placement,
- why you think you should be offered the placement.

Health and safety

As you get older, you need to start taking more responsibility for yourself and for other people. It's important to be aware of health and safety issues, especially when you are on a work placement and are less experienced than those around you.

The law

According to the Health and Safety at Work Act, employers must:

- maintain safe systems of work
- ensure the safe use, handling, storage and transport of articles and substances
- provide adequate instruction, training and supervision
- maintain safe premises and a safe working environment.

And employees must:

- take reasonable care of their own health and safety, and that of others
- cooperate with their employers and others
- not interfere with or misuse anything provided to protect their health and safety, e.g. equipment and protective clothing.

 1 What is meant by 'safe systems of work'? Can you give an example?

2 Do you think the employers should be responsibility for health and safety at work, or the employee? Or should it be shared equally? Give reasons for your views.

 3 Look at the office environment. Where do you think health and safety issues are not being attended to?

Look at the list of occupations below.

- garage mechanic
- hairdresser
- gardener
- shop assistant.

List some health and safety issues you should be aware of if you were a) the employer, and b) the employee.

The facts

- Thousands of young people have accidents at work every year. Some of them are fatal.
- According to the Trade Union Congress, 10 young workers are seriously injured at work every week because they are not aware of their basic health and safety rights as an employee, and have not been given adequate training by their employers.
- Many injuries result from contact with moving machinery, moving objects (including vehicles), and while handling, lifting and carrying things (manual handling).

FOR YOUR FILE

Think about your own work experience placement. Write a paragraph stating health and safety risks you should be concerned about, and what precautions you should take.

Getting started on work experience

Work experience essentials

Before your placement

Think about, and then note down, what you can offer on your placement, and what you'd like to achieve. Then carry out some research. Try and answer the following questions:

- What does your chosen company do?
- How big is it?
- What kinds of jobs do the people working there do?
- What are the working hours?
- What should you wear? Will you need special clothing or can you just dress smartly?
- How will you get there? How long will the journey take and how much will it cost?
- Will you need to take your own lunch or is there a canteen? How much money will you need to take with you for lunch?
- Work out how much money you will need for transport and food every day.

During your placement

There are some simple things to remember when on your placement, whether you decide you'd like to work for that particular company in the future or not:

- Be polite and considerate. Remember, you never know when you'll meet someone you were rude to again. They might be interviewing you for a job in a few years' time!
- Arrive on time and leave only when you are supposed to.
- Try to avoid sitting doing nothing. If you have time to spare, offer to help someone else.
- Make sure you are keen and helpful, and take care not to join in with office gossip.
- Dress appropriately. If you are in an office you will probably need to wear smart clothes. Other jobs may require you to tie back your hair, to remove/cover ear or nose studs, or to wear protective clothing.
- And don't forget to smile!

Finally, remember that work experience is there to help you – so watch your colleagues, learn from them and don't be afraid to ask questions. Even if the job is not the one for you, it will offer you lots of experiences that will help you decide what you want to do in the future.

After your placement

- Write down what you've learned and the training you've received. Include how you managed your time and your workload, and how you overcame any problems. Include this summary on your progress file and/or CV.
- Ask for detailed feedback from your supervisor and ask them if they'll be a reference on your CV.
- Keep in touch with the people you've met – they can let you know about other opportunities in the future.

 ❶ **Discuss what you have learned about work experience essentials.**

❷ **Which are the most useful pieces of advice? Compile a group list of five top tips and share it with the class, giving your reasons.**

The employer's report

When you have finished your work experience, your employer will report back to the school, using a form like the one below. The information in this report will go into your Progress File, so it is important to achieve the best report possible.

Work Experience Employer's Report

Student name: Angela Butt	Form: IOW	Placement name: Touchwood Sports Ltd

Placement address: High Street, Mansfield

Competences: Please indicate student completence using the levels 1 to 4:

1 = competent without help	2 = competent with some help	3 = competent with a great deal of help given	4 = cannot cope at present	N/A = not applicable

a	Responding appropriately with clients	2	i	Follow instructions	3
b	Responding appropriately with supervisor	1	j	Following tasks through to the end	3
c	Responding appropriately with colleagues	2	k	Making independent decisions, showing initiative	2
d	Dealing constructively with criticism	4	l	Demonstrating appropriate attendance and punctuality	1
e	Working with others: team work	4	m	Demonstrating dependability	2
f	Working alone	2	n	Dealing with problems	2
g	Demonstrating appropriate appearance and manner	1	o	Asking questions when in doubt	3
h	Demonstrating interest and enthusiasm	1	p	Learning new things	2

Please give an overview of the student's achievements:

Name: Valerie Childs	Signature: VChilds	
Position: Supervisor		Date: 3/5/05

Read Angela's work experience progress report above. Discuss how well she has done on her placement. What are her strengths and weaknesses? What advice would you give her?

Think of your own work experience placement. Which of areas on the work experience report do you think you will find difficult? What could you do about these areas to make sure you get a good report from your employer? Write a paragraph detailing your thoughts.

12 MANAGING YOUR MONEY

Budgeting

Aim: To explore the world of borrowing, credit and debt, so as to be able to make informed and prudent choices when thinking about borrowing money (PSHE 1e)

"It's not important."

"I'll worry about it tomorrow."

"I've got no idea where to start."

"It's too scary to look at."

 Discuss the fears that teenagers have about managing their money. Do you have the same fears or different ones?

School leavers can't budget

Today's typical school leavers know the cost of a computer game but have no idea how to budget for food, rent and bills, according to new research published today.

In a worrying reflection of teenager priorities, (26%) believe that when they eventually flee the family nest, one of their three biggest expenses will be the cost of going out. 24% believe clothes will absorb the bulk of their budget, and

20% cite expenditure on their mobile phone bills. Nearly (31%) say they are worried about eventually getting into debt.

The survey of 15- and 16-year-old school leavers reveals that 85% know the average cost of a CD, 80% a computer game and 83% a can of cola. But 75% don't know the cost of a colour TV licence and 49% estimate that a new basic fridge would cost more than £200.

FROM A REPORT BY REBECCA SMITHERS, 29 APRIL 2002, WWW.EDUCATIONGUARDIAN.CO.UK

---

 ❶ Are you surprised at the findings in the news article 'School leavers can't budget'? How much does (a) a colour TV licence, (b) a basic fridge, cost?

❷ Discuss what you think the three biggest expenses will be when you leave home.

Allowances

An allowance is an important stepping stone between the pocket money that you received as a child and the student grant or wage that you will have to manage when you leave school.

The first thing you have to do is to negotiate with your parents over how much allowance you should have and what it should cover.

The more items you are expected to pay for, the bigger your allowance should be. If, after a couple of months, you are really struggling to make ends meet, don't be afraid to go back to your parents and renegotiate.

❶ Discuss the advantages and disadvantages of having a monthly rather than weekly allowance.

❷ Design a questionnaire to find out the views of students in your class on allowances. For example, ask: Do you have an allowance? How much is it? What does it cover?

- ☐ Books and magazines
- ☐ CDs
- ☐ Clothes
- ☐ Computer games
- ☐ Driving lessons
- ☐ Food/drink (when out)
- ☐ Going out with friends
- ☐ Films, concerts, etc.
- ☐ Hobbies/sports equipment
- ☐ Make-up/toiletries
- ☐ Presents
- ☐ Savings
- ☐ Sweets
- ☐ Travel

How to budget

If you are wondering why you are always running out of money before the end of the week, then the chances are that you are not budgeting properly. (It could also be that you don't have enough money in the first place, in which case you should ask your parents for a bigger allowance or get a Saturday job!)

Budgeting is a posh word for taking control of your own finances. You do this by calculating, over a set period of time, the following:

- how much money you earn (called income)
- how much money you spend (called outgoings or expenditure)
- how much you save.

Your first attempt at a budget could look like this:

Item	(A) Weekly income (£)	(B) Weekly outgoings (£)	(C) Savings (£)
Allowance/pocket money	16		
Paper round	12		
Karate lessons		7	
Going out		10	
Saving for clothes			5
Food and drink		5	
CDs and other treats		4	
Other savings			5
TOTALS	28	26	10

If it does, you're in trouble! The totals for columns B and C – the money you are either spending or saving – come to £36 altogether. This is £8 more than your income (column A). To balance your budget, you must either increase your income or decrease the amount you spend or save.

You could decide to postpone starting karate lessons and begin saving for them, and reduce your 'other savings' slightly. Your budget would then look like this:

Item	(A) Weekly income (£)	(B) Weekly outgoings (£)	(C) Savings (£)
Allowance/pocket money	16		
Paper round	12		
Karate lessons			2
Going out		10	
Saving for clothes			4
Food and drink		5	
CDs and other treats		4	
Other savings			3
TOTALS	28	19	9

The totals for your outgoings and savings (columns B and C) now equal your income (column A), so your budget is balanced.

If you follow this method and keep a regular account of how you spend your money, you will be able to manage your finances. Otherwise they will manage you.

Work out three other ways in which the budget above could have been balanced. Which is the best way and why? Be prepared to present your conclusions to the rest of the class.

"I get a really good allowance from my parents, but it never seems to last more than a couple of weeks. I'm always asking them for more money, which irritates them, and I never know what I'm going to be able to afford." *Chris, 16*

Write a reply to Chris, advising him on how to manage his money better.

How to manage your finances

Aim: To understand what bank accounts are, what advantages they have and how bank accounts and plastic cards work (PSHE 1e)

Bank accounts and saving

Why do I need a bank account?

Banks and building societies offer a variety of different accounts. Nearly everyone needs an account to help them manage their day-to-day money. It is possible to manage your money using just cash, but putting your money in a bank account can have several advantages.

Bank accounts are safe and convenient. They can help you to:

- **pay bills** – regular payments that you have to make, e.g. electricity bills, can be paid automatically from your bank account by direct debit

- **manage your money** – when your money is in the bank you are less tempted to spend it on impulse. Regular statements allow you to keep track of your income and expenditure

- **receive money** – cheques can be paid directly into your account. This is often how you are paid wages, student loans and benefits

- **keep your money safe** – cash can easily be lost or stolen

- **earn interest** – add a small percentage of the amount in your account

What kind of bank account should I have?

The two main sorts of bank accounts are:

1 **Current accounts** – suitable for managing your day-to-day finances

2 **Savings accounts** – better for longer term savings.

Current accounts

As banks don't let people under the age of 18 borrow money, you will probably be offered a basic bank account. Even if you are older, this type of current account is a good idea if you find it difficult to control your spending.

If you're not careful, you could spend more money than you have in your bank account. This is called going overdrawn; effectively you are borrowing from the bank.

Savings accounts

A savings account is for your spare cash, so that you can save it up and earn a higher rate of interest. But you can't use it for spending so you won't get a cheque book or plastic card.

You will still be able to withdraw the money if you really have to, but you will probably then lose some of the extra interest.

FROM *YOUNG CITIZENS' PASSPORT*

Features of a basic bank account

A cash card – so you can take money out at a cash machine, but you can't withdraw more than you have in your account.

A Solo or Electron debit card – which you can use to pay for things in many shops, by phone and over the internet. With some debit cards, like Solo and Electron, your account is checked before each transaction and goes ahead only if there is enough in your account to meet the payment.

Direct debits – which enable regular bills to be paid automatically direct from your account.

Direct credits – which enable regular payments (such as wages or your student loan) to be paid direct into your account automatically.

FROM WWW.FSA.GOV.UK/CONSUMER/TEACHING/INDEX.HTML

What are the advantages of opening a bank account? Which do you think are the three most important reasons, and why?

Discuss reasons you may have for saving money. Think of short-term and long-term reasons, and include saving 'for a rainy day', as well as for planned items or events.

FOR YOUR FILE

A friend has gone overdrawn on their current account, but has plenty of money in a savings account. Write a letter to them advising what they should do, including ways to avoid going overdrawn on their current account.

Plastic – Your flexible friend

You're in town and Byrite are having a massive sale. You need cash quick, but didn't bring enough out. What you need is a way of getting money out of your bank without the hassle of filling in forms. You need 'plastic'!

Since you were little, you've probably wanted one – whether it's to save keeping your money under the bed or to make your wallet/purse look a little more impressive. However, there are several types of plastic banking cards that serve different purposes – some for plain cash withdrawal from machines, or others for ordering that full set of James Bond videos off the internet.

Cheque guarantee card: If you want to pay for goods by cheque from your current account, you'll probably need one of these to back up your cheque.

Cash card: Gets you cash from the holes in the wall, or ATMs (Automated Teller Machines).

Debit card: This works like a combined cheque and cheque guarantee card, taking the money out of your account when you pay for your goods.

Charge card: Any store card is usually a charge card. You get a set limit and you have to pay off a minimum amount towards it each month.

Credit card: Credit cards allow you to spend money you don't have without any interest being charged on it for a certain length of time. However, if you don't pay it off in time, the interest on your 'borrowed' money will go up and cost you more. That's why you usually have to be over 18 or 21, before you get one.

FROM PUPILINE

Discuss what you have learned about managing your finances. Write a short definition for each of the following:

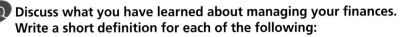

- current account
- savings account
- cheque book
- debit card
- interest
- cashpoint machine.

13 HEALTHY EATING

Eating and dieting

Aim: To explore attitudes to body shape, eating and dieting, and to explain what are healthy eating habits (PSHE 2a, 2d)

What teenage girls think about their bodies

Bliss magazine surveyed 2,000 girls, aged between 10 and 19 years old, about their attitudes to their bodies. They discovered:

- 87% of teenage girls were unhappy with their body
- 56% of the girls interviewed thought "If I was thinner, I'd be happier".

Are you body happy?

Over half the teenage girls in the survey who describe their bodies as average thought they needed to lose weight. Unfortunately, it's become scarily normal to think that being average size isn't good enough. Everyone wants to be skinny.

love your body!

When we look in the mirror we usually focus on the bits we hate and ignore the rest. "Look at the whole person, not just one area," says Jade McEwan from the Eating Disorders Association.

What would you do to lose weight?

19% of the teenage girls interviewed had an eating disorder and 26% had considered diet pills and plastic surgery. Teenage bodies don't finish developing until their 20s – why do girls want to mess around with them now?

love your body!

"Experts know that on the whole 'diets' don't work long-term," says psychologist Dr Liao. "It's more important to eat healthy food regularly and exercise."

Do you think 'thin' means 'popular'?

A massive 72% of the girls reckoned that thin girls are more popular. Almost all of the girls who claimed to be overweight believed they'd have more friends and lad interest if they were skinny!

love your body!

"Many girls buy into a 'thin fantasy', believing that if only they were thinner, lots of things would change," says Dr Liao. "In fact, the only thing that changes is your clothes size. Remind yourself that you don't need to be satisfied with your body to like your life. Then work on loving your body."

Don't think thin – think healthy

Helen Johnston, the Editor of *Bliss*, says: "Female body image obsession has reached epidemic proportions. Teenage girls look to their mums for guidance, only to see many of them continually worrying about their own body shape and size.

Now many girls of 13 and 14 are dieting constantly at an age when their bodies are still developing. They need to stop thinking thin and start thinking healthy, and learn that confidence is much sexier than thin legs."

FROM *BLISS*

What the celebs say

"I finally realised I don't have an A-plus perfect body – but I'm very happy and I'm not going to worry about a few extra pounds. Puppy fat is sexy."

Drew Barrymore

"I couldn't care less about stupid diets. Eating is sensual and fun. I'm not going to let it be spoiled by calorie counting."

Christina Aguilera

❶ Discuss what you have learned from the survey about teenage girls' attitudes to their bodies, to eating and to dieting.

❷ Do you think teenagers are obsessed with their body images? Where do you think the pressure comes from?

What do you think?

"You can't be attractive unless you're very thin."

"Thin people are more popular."

"Exercise is a better way of controlling your weight than dieting."

"It's more important to eat properly than to try to lose weight."

"How you look matters more than what sort of person you are."

 Discuss each statement, saying whether you agree or disagree with it, and why.

Develop healthy eating habits

Top tips to healthy eating

The whole world seems diet obsessed. Young adults are currently facing a huge weight crisis in the UK. Recent figures show that over 75% of 11 to 16-year-olds don't exercise, and that rates of teen obesity are rising. It seems most girls are either starving themselves or eating so unhealthily they're overweight.

And the answer? Do some exercise and eat more healthily. Because a balanced diet will boost your energy levels, improve your complexion, help build up bones and your immune system, and help you lose weight if you need to.

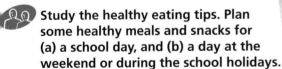 Study the healthy eating tips. Plan some healthy meals and snacks for (a) a school day, and (b) a day at the weekend or during the school holidays.

Seven top eating tips

1 **Don't cut the carbs completely.** Your body needs carbohydrates, just like it needs protein and vitamins, so fill up on rice, pasta, wholemeal bread, spuds and cereals.

2 **Blitz zits** – by eating five portions of fruit and veg each day. They're packed with vital vitamins that'll give you clear, glowing skin and shiny, silky hair.

3 **Don't ditch the dairy** – milk, cheese and yoghurt are all packed with bone-building calcium, and because you don't stop growing until you're 18, it's something you need.

4 **Get plenty of protein** – meat, chicken, fish, eggs and beans all help to build and repair cells. Have two portions a day and snack on protein-rich nuts and seeds.

5 **Cut down on fatty and sugary foods** – but don't cut them out altogether. A little bit of everything is good for you and if you deny yourself something totally, you'll just crave it even more.

6 **Don't diet** – starving yourself of calories is definitely not a smart way to lose weight. Instead, eat regularly and exercise for an hour at least three times a week.

7 **Be water wise** – drink at least eight glasses a day. Water keeps you fit and active, while soft and sugary drinks actually steal water from the body to process the sugar.

FROM *BLISS*

Anorexia – the facts

Rather than making you thin and attractive, starving yourself will make you thin and ill. A person who deliberately avoids eating, or eats very little, in order to keep their weight below a healthy level, has the eating condition known as 'anorexia nervosa'. Over 70,000 people in Britain have the condition and one in 10 sufferers is a boy.

People with anorexia are not getting enough energy, so they feel tired and weak. They constantly feel cold and sometimes soft, fine hairs grow on their bodies to protect them. A girl with anorexia may stop having her periods and her bones may become brittle. Severe anorexia can cause a dangerous loss of minerals in the body fluids. In extreme cases it can lead to death.

"I feel I'm overweight, so I'm thinking of going on a crash diet. My friend says it's the only thing that works. Is she right?"

Marvina

 Discuss this letter to a problem page in a teenage magazine and draft a reply. For further information, contact Eating Disorders Association: www.edauk.com or ANRED (Anorexia Nervosa and Related Eating Disorders): www.anred.com

Healthy eating and junk food

Aim: To examine why many teenagers do not eat healthily, and to discuss how far junk foods are responsible for making people overweight (PSHE 2a, 2d)

Teenagers are getting less fit

Health experts say teenagers are less fit than they used to be. What has caused this drop in fitness? Most health experts believe there are two factors:

1 A change in eating habits. There's a greater reliance on fast foods, junk foods and ready meals, rather than on a healthy, balanced diet of three regular meals a day.

2 A decline in the amount of exercise taken. We travel more by car, bus or train rather than walking or cycling, and spend time watching TV or on the computer rather than on outdoor activities that would use up excess fat.

Teenagers 'too idle' to bother with good food

Teenagers know which foods are good for them, but cannot be bothered to eat healthily or learn to cook properly, according to a survey. Although three-quarters associate a good diet with long-term health, few can make more than toast, and most choose crisps and chocolates rather than fruit.

Among those who do eat fruit, laziness puts them off anything that requires peeling. "If we buy grapes, I eat loads and loads," a 17-year-old boy said. "Oranges you have to peel and that's a chore."

Four out of ten teenagers surveyed did not eat breakfast. Almost half ate at a fast food restaurant at least once a week, more out of idleness and a desire for convenience than for any other reason.

When they arrive at school, few teenagers eat healthily. Only one in six buys fruit, vegetables or yoghurts. "In the morning I have cereal," a 17-year-old boy said. "But sometimes I can't be bothered so I just have a drink. At breaktime I might have three chocolate bars or a burger. Today I had a burger."

Diets worsen at weekends and during holidays. A 16-year-old girl was typical of the two in five teenagers who miss breakfast because they stay

in bed. She said: "At weekends or in the holidays I don't usually eat until the evening because I sleep more during the day."

Few teenagers associate eating with regular meal times and most lack the skill to prepare anything more than a ready meal. While six out of 10 knew how to use a microwave, fewer than a quarter had ever made a pasta sauce.

FROM *THE DAILY TELEGRAPH*

 ❶ Discuss whether you think the newspaper report is fair to teenagers. How accurate are the statements it makes? Do you know which foods are good for you? Are most teenagers unable to cook anything other than toast or ready meals? Are teenagers too lazy to eat properly?

❷ Plan and carry out your own survey on teenagers' eating habits. Report your findings to the rest of the class and say whether they support the findings of the survey reported in the article.

Obesity – storing up problems for the future

The number of people who are obese (extremely overweight) has increased dramatically in the past 25 years in the UK. Obesity is a problem not only for adults, but for young people too.

Britain has some of the highest proportions of overweight young people for a developed country. Already 8.5% of six-year-olds and 15% of 15-year-olds are classed as obese.

Young people who are obese are storing up problems for the future. Overweight teenagers often become overweight adults, and obesity can cause serious health problems – heart disease, diabetes, circulation problems, high blood pressure and joint problems.

Each year, obesity costs the NHS £3 billion and causes 30,000 premature deaths.

Q. How can I tell if I'm overweight?

A. There's no such thing as an ideal weight for everybody, because people are different shapes and sizes. For example, some people are naturally stocky, while others have a narrower frame. Also, while you're a teenager, your body shape is still changing. So if you're worried about being overweight, talk to your doctor. Don't rely on charts for height and weight. They're meant for adults.

What can be done?

Junk food adverts to be banned in crackdown on obesity

The government's top food adviser is considering harsh laws to ban junk food advertising and prevent firms from using celebrities to endorse products high in fat, sugar and salt.

The chairman of the Food Standards Agency warned that if the number of overweight young people was not reduced, life expectancy could start to fall.

In addition to possible bans on junk food advertising, other measures under consideration include:

- pressurising supermarkets to offer 'buy one, get one free' promotions only on healthy children's foods
- making shops replace sweets on sale at checkouts with healthier options
- labelling products that are high in fat, sugar or salt clearly on the front of packets, possibly in the form of a government health warning
- banning vending machines from stocking sweets and crisps in schools and leisure centres
- putting a 'fat tax' on cakes, biscuits and processed food.

FROM *THE SUNDAY TIMES*

Put VAT on high-fat food, urges GP

Doctors are calling for a new 'fat tax' on cakes, biscuits and processed food to tackle obesity.

A British Medical Association conference is to debate if 17.5% VAT should be added to all high-fat food.

Because most food is exempt from VAT, extending the tax would raise millions of pounds.

Dr Martin Breach, who is proposing the new tax, believes the money would cover the cost of treating the health problems caused by obesity and might also change people's behaviour.

FROM *THE DAILY TELEGRAPH*

❶ How far do you think junk foods are to blame for increases in obesity?

❷ Discuss the proposed measures to reduce the problem of obesity. Which ones do you think would be effective?

14 SAFER SEX AND CONTRACEPTION

When is the right time to have sex?

Aim: To discuss what you need to consider when deciding whether or not to have sex with someone, to explore attitudes towards sex and how to resist unwanted pressure (PSHE 2a, 2b, 2e, 2f, 3b)

Sex and you – waiting until the time is right

The age of consent, the age when it is legal for a young person to have sex, is 16. Some young people have sex before they are 14. Some young people wait until they are older than 16. Many relationships build slowly: the couple become good friends, getting to become close mentally and then, perhaps, physically. Some young people are keen to explore the physical side sooner rather than later and the question of sex crops up – do you or don't you?

The most important thing to remember at this time is never be pressurised into anything you know you're not ready for, and that goes for all things, sexual or not!

Think about the following:

- Sex, once given, cannot be taken back.
- Moral aspects – some cultures and religions believe that remaining a virgin until after marriage is very important. Would you feel guilty or cause trouble if you disobey your beliefs?
- Giving the most intimate part of yourself to someone else should be a thought-out, loving and valued experience by both people involved. It should feel 'right' and without guilt.
- Everyone does not 'do it', despite what they might claim. If you want to wait until you are sure, that is your right and choice.

Sex needs to be discussed between the two of you. Some couples want to take things slowly, especially if they're both young, or they plan to save a full sexual relationship until after marriage. Many religions still maintain that sex is only morally right when you're in a marriage, and you should not have sex before getting married. Some cultures believe that this makes for mutual respect, faithfulness and true love.

Other couples believe sex and intimacy is an important part of their relationship and believe they're mature enough to handle it. It just depends on you, your circumstances, and how much you feel about the other person. There is plenty of exploring of each other's bodies which can be enjoyed without having to 'go all the way' and have full penetrative sex.

FROM *BUT YOU DON'T UNDERSTAND* BY ELAINE SISHTON AND CHARLOTTE RUSSELL

What do you think?

"I'm worried s/he will leave me if I don't agree."

"We've discussed it and it's something we both want to do."

"Everyone else is doing it."

"When I'm drunk, I can't stop myself. I'll do anything with anyone."

"I just want to find out what it's like."

❶ **What do you think of these reasons for having sex? Discuss each one in turn.**

❷ **Some people think the age of consent should be lowered from 16 to 14. Discuss the arguments for and against.**

Sex = love?

Sex isn't the same thing as love in the true sense of the word. Sex can be self-centred and a purely physical and selfish craving. There are people who see the opposite sex as just 'bodies' to be used. Don't deceive yourself into thinking that people really care for you when all they want is sex. The truth is that they probably don't care for you as much as you would like. Hormones are flying high in the teenage years, and people feel they want to experiment.

There is a lot of pressure and gossip amongst groups as to who has 'done it', when and with whom. Boys in particular may try to blackmail girls into having sex, and will try every trick and persuasive argument they can think of. Don't be conned into doing something you may later regret. Respect yourself and your own body. Take no notice of pressure from other people – it is your decision alone.

Protection

If you do decide an active sex life is right for you, then there are a few important things to consider. The main one is risk. Pregnancy or sexually transmitted infections (STIs), such as genital herpes or chlamydia, are real dangers to be considered. Protect yourself by:

- not having sex
- avoiding situations you may find it difficult to get out of, such as getting drunk at a party and not being able to think clearly

- sticking to one partner (the more partners you have, the more chance you have of catching a sexually transmitted infection)
- using condoms (although not 100% safe, these significantly reduce the dangers).

FROM *BUT YOU DON'T UNDERSTAND* BY ELAINE SISHTON AND CHARLOTTE RUSSELL

Resisting pressure

You can resist all kinds of pressure if you give your own preferences priority.

> "I know you've got your values, but I've got mine, and they're important to me."

> "It's very easy to have sex, but I want more than that."

> "An orgasm isn't everything."

> "It's childish not to consider the consequences of having sex."

FROM *SEX ED* BY DR MIRIAM STOPPARD

1 Discuss how you would explain to a partner that being in love doesn't mean you have to have sex. How would you say 'No'?

2 How helpful do you find the responses Dr Miriam Stoppard suggests? Can you suggest any other responses?

Practising safer sex

Aim: To understand methods of contraception and how to practise safer sex, and to discuss unplanned pregnancies (PSHE 2a, 2b, 2e, 2f, 3b)

What is safer sex?

All sex involves some risk. That's why people refer to 'safer' sex rather than 'safe' sex. Practising safer sex means taking precautions to protect yourself against an unplanned pregnancy or catching a sexually transmitted infection (STI). It means avoiding risky sexual practices that could harm you, either physically or emotionally.

The lowdown on... contraception

If you're considering having sex, you need to think about contraception first. The most popular forms of contraception for young people are condoms and the Pill. There are also female condoms and hormone injections, which should be discussed with your GP.

The Pill
There are two types – the mini pill (containing the hormone progestogen) and the combined pill (containing oestrogen and progestogen). The Pill is 99% effective against pregnancy but does not protect against STIs. For more information, see page 71.

Condoms
When placed over a hard penis, condoms trap sperm when a boy ejaculates. They're 98% effective against pregnancy and can protect against STIs. Look for condoms with the CE and British kitemark symbols; use them once only and note the expiry date. Oil-based products (baby oil and Vaseline) can damage condoms, as can nails or jewellery.

Emergency contraception (morning after pill)
If a contraceptive method fails, emergency contraception pills can help. They can be used up to 72 hours after sex, but the sooner they're taken the better. The pills are available free from GPs, family planning clinics, Brook Centres and NHS walk-in centres. They are also available from pharmacies (for over 16s) and cost £24.

❶ Discuss the arguments for and against this view and say why you agree or disagree with it.

"The morning after pill should be available in all schools confidentially to anyone who asks for it, whatever their age."

❷ In a few years' time it may be possible for men to have a hormonal contraceptive implanted under the arm which would last for a year. Do you think men would want to use this method? Who should take responsibility for contraception – the man or the woman?

Real life
Jasmine, 17, has a long-term boyfriend and is taking the Pill.

"I've been with my boyfriend for seven months and I'm on the Pill now. I started taking it for contraception and because it helped clear up my bad skin.

Before I was on the Pill, I had a scare when the condom we were using split. I tried not to panic and went to the chemist where I got the morning after pill. I think being able to buy emergency contraception over the counter is great because there is less of a negative stigma now.

If you're considering having sex, always carry condoms – regardless of your age. If you ask me, I think it's irresponsible not to, especially with the rise in STIs. Condoms protect you from STIs and the Pill won't do that. If a lad won't use one, dump him – he doesn't care about you."

FROM *LET'S TALK ABOUT SEX*, J17

FOR YOUR FILE

"My girlfriend's going on the Pill. Do I still need to use a condom?"

K

Draft a reply to K's letter.

What you need to know about the Pill

The Pill can:

- ease period pains
- make your period lighter and more regular
- stop bad premenstrual stress (PMS) moods
- prevent pregnancy.

But only if you take it correctly. According to a study, two out of every three girls who are on the Pill don't take it as directed. The Pill is not error-proof. Talk to your GP and read the directions on the Pill packet for more advice.

Here are some things anyone on the Pill must know...

- Being sick or having diarrhoea, or taking antibiotics and some other medicines may stop the Pill from working.
- The Pill is most effective if you take it at the same time each day.

FROM *COSMO GIRL*

The lowdown on... pregnancy

Get sussed before you get serious

If you've ever had sex or thought about it, one of your biggest concerns might be the risk of getting pregnant.

First things first. What some girls don't realise is that if sperm come into contact with the vagina in any way, there is a risk of getting pregnant. This means that if a lad has sperm on his fingers he should keep them away from your privates. You can also fall pregnant if you have sex during your period.

The best way to avoid pregnancy is to never have sexual contact without a reliable method of contraception, regardless of the time of the month.

If you miss a period and think you might be pregnant (bear in mind that periods can be erratic in your teens), you should take a pregnancy test as soon as possible. It is important to find out if you're pregnant or not, so that you have time to consider all your options.

What if I'm pregnant?

Facing an unplanned pregnancy is difficult at any age, but can be even more distressing if you're under 16 and may not know what options are available to you. It's common to feel shocked, confused, embarrassed, isolated or lonely when facing an unplanned pregnancy.

Remember – you are not alone. If you feel unable to talk to your family or boyfriend, professionals are there to provide information and support. Once you have been advised of the options, you can make a decision about what's best for you.

The options open to a girl who is under 16 years old and gets pregnant are:

- keep the baby
- have the baby adopted
- have an abortion.

Discuss these options. What are the key factors that should influence her decision? How much say should the boy who is the father or her parents have? What are the arguments for and against having an abortion?

Real life

Susie, 19, felt confused and upset when she discovered she was pregnant.

"I was on the Pill when I fell pregnant. No one told me that if you're sick it can affect the Pill and it may not be as effective. After I started getting stomach pains I went to see the doctor, and when he told me I was pregnant I couldn't believe it. My boyfriend burst into tears when I told him, but said he'd stick by whatever decision I made. After professional advice we agreed that having an abortion was best as we felt too young to take on the responsibility of a child.

In December I went to hospital to have the abortion. The doctor gave me a tablet to take and a few days later I went back to be given a pill internally. It wasn't pleasant, but I knew it was the right thing for me. You can never be too careful when it comes to contraception. Prevention is the best thing."

FROM *J17*

FOR YOUR FILE

Write a story about a teenage girl who becomes pregnant. Explain what decision she makes and why.

15 DRINKING AND SMOKING

Understanding why people drink

Aim: To discuss why people drink, to understand the risks of binge drinking, and to explore ways of drinking sensibly (PSHE 2a, 2b, 2e)

Alcohol – what's the attraction?

Alcohol plays a big part in our world, with over 90% of adults enjoying a drink on a regular basis. That doesn't make it compulsory for you to drink alcohol, but understanding the reasons for the appeal could help you to drink sensibly.

The buzz

Like any drug, alcohol affects your mood. In small amounts, it can help people loosen up, so they feel chatty and less self-conscious. The problems only kick in if you turn to drink because it seems like the only way to have a good time, or because you're uptight, bored or lacking the self-confidence just to be yourself when sober.

The image

OK, so hard drinking has a macho appeal. We're led to believe that a real man can drink without dropping, while our action movie heroes are often seen steadying their nerves with a drop of the strong stuff. In reality, if you drink to get drunk, the end result is always the same. You might have a good time up to a point, but after that you risk spinning out of control, vomiting or just doing something you badly regret. It doesn't impress, and nor will it leave you feeling good about yourself. Inside every 'hard drinker' you'll find an individual with personal problems he can't sort out because booze has got the better of him.

FROM *XY: A TOOLKIT FOR LIFE* BY MATT WHYMAN

GETTING TRASHED – THE RISKS

- You may get alcohol poisoning and end up in hospital. Several teenagers die each year from acute alcohol poisoning or from choking on their own vomit.
- You are more likely to pick an argument and get into a fight.
- You are more likely to have an accident. 40% of visits to hospital casualty departments are drink-related, rising to 70% at weekends.
- You may find yourself having sex with someone you'd rather not have had sex with. You may not use a condom, risking an unwanted pregnancy or STI.
- You may do something stupid and commit a criminal offence. You may get arrested and with a police record.
- Teenagers who drink excessive amounts are likely to have poor eating habits, more respiratory problems, general fatigue and sleep disorders.
- Regularly drinking too much means you risk becoming dependent on alcohol.
- Long-term heavy drinkers can damage their livers and develop cirrhosis.

 ❶ Discuss the views below. What would you say to someone that said that to you?

❷ Plan a video to warn young people of the dangers of binge-drinking. Take turns to present your plans to the rest of the class.

> "We go out to get wrecked. It's a laugh."

> "People who don't drink are killjoys."

> "A person who's drunk is a real turn-off."

> "There's lots of ways of having a good night out without getting trashed."

FOR YOUR FILE

"Dear Erica,

I am worried about my brother, who's 17. He's started binge-drinking. What are the risks? What can I say to him to get him to stop?"

Taz

Write a reply to Taz's letter.

The risks of binge drinking

Put an end to 'happy hours'

The bars that cope with competition by offering cheap, reckless promos are not taking their responsibilities as licensees seriously. 'Happy hours' introduce a time pressure to get the best value, and people who get drunk early on tend to continue.

FROM *THE GUARDIAN*

Doctors call for health warnings on alcohol

Doctors are concerned about the effects of the spreading habit of binge drinking in young people. They propose that the labels on all drinks containers should say: 'HM Government Health Warning. This product contains [x] units of alcohol. Consumption of more than 21 units per week for men and 14 units per week for women can damage your health.'

FROM *THE DAILY TELEGRAPH*

Ban TV adverts 'glorifying' drink, say doctors

Doctors have called for a ban on television advertising of alcohol in an attempt to stem the rising tide of binge drinking by young people. They say "We all agree that in moderation it is a good thing, but adverts don't say 'have a glass or two'. Alcohol harms and we want to see the glorification of it on our television screens ended."

FROM *THE DAILY TELEGRAPH*

Measures to cut down binge drinking

- Don't allow under 18s into bars after 8pm.
- Ban TV adverts that 'glorify' drink.
- Put health warnings on all alcoholic drinks.
- Ban promotions such as 'happy hours'.
- Increase on-the-spot fines for drunkenness.
- Make young people who are found drunk and disorderly attend alcohol-education classes.

 Discuss the suggestions above. Which do you think would be most effective? What other measures can you suggest?

Ways to drink sensibly

Drinking isn't compulsory – you can choose not to booze. Being smart about alcohol means thinking ahead, so here are some tips to be sure that alcohol doesn't get the better of you.

- Eat a decent meal before you go out. Starchy stuff, like bread, potatoes and pasta, and fatty food such as chips, can take a while to digest and will help absorb alcohol.
- Aim to enjoy a drink as part of the social setting, but to respect your limits. If you're not sure what you can handle, take it easy. You'll soon learn where to draw the line.
- Pace yourself. Give your body a chance to process the alcohol from one drink to the next. Also sip each drink instead of swigging it down.
- Alternate alcohol with water and a non-alcoholic, non-fizzy drink now and then.
- Avoid mixing drinks. Different types of booze mean more toxins to deal with. As a result you may find you stop enjoying yourself and start wishing you hadn't had that last drink.

FROM *XY: A TOOLKIT FOR LIFE* BY MATT WHYMAN

 Study the information on how to be smart about drinking. Write down the reasons for each piece of advice.

Understanding why people smoke

Aim: To understand how smoking and passive smoking can damage your health, and to discuss techniques that can be used to resist unhelpful pressure to smoke or drink (PSHE 2a, 2b, 2e)

Smoking – what's the attraction?

The smoking lifestyle

Lighting up is often viewed as an act of rebellion, and even sophistication. It's a strong image used by the cigarette industry and media to reinforce certain ideas, attitudes and beliefs.

Joining the pack

Peer pressure can be a powerful force, which means if your mates are lighting up, then you might find it hard to resist. Much depends on your self-esteem – if you feel confident in yourself, then you are less likely to light up.

Mood control

Nicotine in tobacco is a powerful and fast-acting drug that has a stimulating effect on the body. Even so, many people believe that reaching for the cigarettes helps them stay calm, relieving stress and feelings of nervousness.

FROM *XY: A TOOLKIT FOR LIFE* BY MATT WHYMAN

The risks

Lighting up	Passive smoking
• 90% of deaths from lung cancer are linked to smoking. It also causes 80% of the deaths from diseases like bronchitis, emphysema and heart disease.	• The immediate effects of passive smoking include eye irritation, headache, cough, sore throat, dizziness and feeling sick. Other people's smoke can reduce coronary blood flow.
• A person who smokes is likely to die between six and nine years younger than a non-smoker.	• 80% of asthma sufferers say tobacco smoke causes them to have breathing difficulties.
• Research suggests that 120,000 men under 50 are sexually impotent because of smoking.	• 17,000 children under five go into hospital each year as a result of their parents smoking.
• Tobacco can stain your teeth and nails, make your skin wrinkled and your breath smell. The smoke gets into your hair and clothes and makes them smell, too.	• Non-smokers who are exposed to passive smoking at home have a 25% increased risk of heart disease and lung cancer.
• Around 5,000 fires a year are caused by smoking-related materials, resulting in about 160 deaths.	• It is estimated that 1,000 people die each year as a result of diseases caused by passive smoking.

 1 Discuss the views below.

"Health warnings on cigarette packets are a waste of time. No one takes any notice."

"The only way to cut down the number of smokers is to raise the price of cigarettes to a level where people can't afford to buy them."

2 Imagine you are a team of advisers appointed by the government to draw up plans for an anti-smoking campaign aimed at teenagers. Draw up your plans and present them to the rest of the class.

FOR YOUR FILE

"Dear Erica

My boyfriend smokes and tells me not to be ridiculous when I say it affects me, too. What can I say to him? I'm afraid if I challenge him, he'll dump me." *Gaby*

Draft a reply to Gaby's letter.

An answer to passive smoking?

Ban smoking in public place, say doctors

Britain's most senior doctors called for a ban on smoking in public places. They estimate that it could save 160,000 lives.

They say most people in Britain are now non-smokers and find cigarette smoke unpleasant.

"We believe the time has come for legislation to make public places smoke-free. Everyone has a right to freedom from tobacco smoke and pollution," the doctors said.

FROM THE DAILY TELEGRAPH

> "Nobody should dictate to anybody whether they smoke, or when and where they smoke."

> "It's my right to breathe smoke-free air. It's smokers who have a problem and they shouldn't share it with non-smokers."

 Some countries, like Ireland, and many cities, like New York, are banning smoking in public places. Look at the quotes above and list the arguments for and against banning smoking in public places. Share your views with the rest of the class.

 Some doctors have called for a total ban on the sale of tobacco. The director of ASH (Action for Smoking and Health) says such a ban is 'neither possible, nor desirable'. What do you think?

Resisting the pressure to smoke

Erica Stewart offers some tips on how to say 'No'

Saying 'No' isn't easy. Don't feel you have to give a long explanation why you don't want to smoke (or have a drink). Try a few of these responses (see below, right).

Don't get drawn into a discussion or an argument, try to change the conversation. Remember, a true friend will respect you enough to accept what you're saying and to leave it to you to make your own decisions, instead of trying to get you to do what they want you to do.

❶ Discuss how some people put pressure on others to either smoke or drink. What sort of things do they say? How would you say 'No'?

❷ How helpful do you find the responses Erica Stewart suggests? Can you suggest any other responses?

> "No, thanks."

> "I just don't feel in the mood for it today."

> "I don't need one right now."

> "I'm in training at the moment."

> "If I smoke, it makes me feel ill."

> "I've tried it and I don't like it."

> "I get an allergic reaction if I have one."

> "I've been told not to because of a condition I have."

16 HEALTH MATTERS

Keeping healthy

Aim: To understand how to take responsibility for your own health, including exploring the importance of not damaging your hearing, and the problems of acne (PSHE 2a, 2g)

Looking after your own health

Now that you're a young adult, it's time for you to take responsibility for your own healthcare.

There are a number of things you need to know so that you can look after your own health.

The more you know about your health, the more you will have the power to make your own choices about how to look after yourself.

 Look at the checklist, right. How many of the questions can you answer? Create your own checklist and do some research to fill in any gaps.

1 *GPs details: the name, address and telephone number of your doctor*

2 *National health card/NHS number and where you keep them*

3 *Immunisations: what you have had and where you keep your immunisation record card*

4 *Illnesses: what illnesses you have had, e.g. mumps, measles, chicken pox, German measles*

5 *Allergies: anything you are allergic to, e.g. medicines, plasters, foods, and how you deal with it*

6 *Medical conditions: details of any medical conditions you may have and any medication you take, e.g. dosage, side effects*

7 *Family history: any medical conditions that are common in your family, e.g. high blood pressure, diabetes*

Look after your hearing

Clubbers warned to wear earplugs or risk deafness

Earplugs should be readily available in dance clubs, deafness campaigners suggested in a report warning that young people were unaware of the damage they might be doing to their hearing.

Clubbers risked encountering hearing loss in middle age rather than old age according to the report published by the Royal National Institute for Deaf People.

A survey found that 62% of young people admitted hearing problems after going to clubs, and 72% reported problems after rock or pop concerts.

Noise levels in clubs were said to range from 95–120 decibels, which compared to 110 decibels for a pneumatic drill and 85 for the threshold at which ear protection is required in industry.

With clubbers often being exposed to more than 100 decibels of music for several hours, the report said it was vital that people took regular breaks from the dance floor and stayed away from music speakers.

Event promoters should provide information on protecting hearing and should encourage use of earplugs.

FROM *THE GUARDIAN*

 ❶ **Discuss the risks of hearing loss from exposure to loud music.**

❷ **Imagine you have been asked to plan a 30-second TV film as part of a health education campaign to try to convince young people who are going clubbing that they need to wear earplugs. Share your ideas for the film with the rest of the class.**

Understanding acne

Don't let acne get you down

Dr Daron Seukeran, a skin specialist, explains what causes acne and how it can be treated

All teenagers dread getting acne. Unfortunately, more than 95% will get it, with a few developing acne before the age of 12, and up to 40% developing it after the age of 16.

What causes acne?

Acne is caused when glands in the skin – that produce the body's natural oil called sebum – seem to become more sensitive to hormones in the body. This leads to an increased amount of sebum being produced. The ducts from these glands to the skin surface become blocked and filled with bacteria which causes inflammation (swelling and redness), resulting in pimples and cysts. This often happens at the time of hormonal changes. Some young women find that acne is worse at particular times of their menstrual cycle.

Myths about acne

Many myths surround acne, such as that eating too much chocolate and greasy food causes acne or makes it worse. There is no evidence to suggest this. The idea that acne is due to 'infection' as a result of poor hygiene is also false and there is no need to wash excessively.

Where to go for help

Don't be embarrassed to seek help just because you think others consider it a trivial problem.

Visit your pharmacist who can help you choose the most suitable 'topical' acne medications that are available 'over the counter'. Topical here means 'applied to the surface of the skin'.

If, after several weeks, there is no improvement, see your GP who may prescribe other 'topical' medications that are only available on prescription. If your acne is more severe, you may be given a course of antibiotics, or girls may be advised to take the contraceptive pill because it helps to balance hormones. If your acne doesn't improve, your doctor may refer you to a dermatologist (skin specialist).

The message is: 'Do not wait to grow out of your spots'. The sooner acne is treated, the better you will feel and the risk of scarring will be decreased. But don't expect instant results. Some treatments can take a while to work, and it's important to finish any course of medication prescribed to you!

FROM *'SPOTLIGHT ON ACNE'* BY DR DARON SEUKERAN

 Share what you have learned about acne. What causes it? Why is it common among teenagers? What are some of the common myths about acne? How can acne be treated?

 Use the internet to find out more about acne. One useful website is: www.skincarephysicians.com/acnenet

FOR YOUR FILE

Draw up a list of 'Ten things you should know about acne' for a teenage magazine.

Health care check

Aim: To examine the health risks of sunbathing, tattooing and body piercing (PSHE 2a, 2e)

Sunbathing – is it worth the risk?

Young people in Britain will face a skin cancer 'time bomb' unless they heed warnings about exposure to the sun and stop their obsessive pursuit of tans, say health experts.

A survey of 16- and 24-year-olds found that more than 70% of them wanted a tan on holiday, despite the risk of potentially fatal skin cancer from ultraviolet (UV) radiation. Unless young people change their habits and learn to protect themselves properly in the sun, we could be heading for a cancer time bomb.

A burning problem

- There are almost 70,000 cases of skin cancer in Britain every year, the most deadly form of which is malignant melanoma. This form causes around 1,700 deaths a year.
- As a result of a 20-year campaign in Australia, the country has about 1,000 skin cancer deaths a year – 700 fewer than Britain!

Sun protection tips

Stay in the shade between 11am and 3pm.

Make sure you never burn.

Cover up with a T-shirt, wide-brimmed hat and sunglasses.

Use factor 15-plus sunscreen.

Melanoma – the facts

- Skin cancers are caused by the ultraviolet radiation (UV) in the sun's rays, which can damage the DNA in your cells.
- A melanoma develops as a new mole that is black or odd-looking, or as an old mole that has changed.
- In men, the most common area for melanomas to appear is on the torso; in women, it is on the legs.
- Malignant melanomas are treatable. They can be surgically removed – an operation that leaves hardly any scarring.

'BINGE' SUNBATHERS RISK THEIR LIVES FOR A TAN

Getting a tan by 'binge' sunbathing at weekends or a two-week holiday abroad significantly increases the risk of getting malignant melanoma, the most deadly form of skin cancer.

The number of melanoma cases is increasing annually, partly due to the British habit of sunbathing in short bursts of intense exposure.

Melanoma is now one of the commonest causes of death in young people.

Bad sunburn in teenage years can push up the chances 13-fold of developing melanoma later, usually between the ages of 40 and 60. People with a large number of moles – more than 100 – have an increased risk.

FROM *THE DAILY MAIL*

 ❶ Discuss what you have learned about the dangers of sunbathing. Why is 'binge sunbathing' so risky?

❷ Design a poster to warn teenagers of the risks of sunbathing and to give them advice on things they can do to reduce the risks.

 Find out more about the prevention, diagnosis and treatment of melanoma from the following website: www.melanoma.com/melanoma/index.jsp

Health care check – tattoos

Tattoos are permanent. That's because the tattooist uses a needle to inject coloured ink deep into your skin. Once it's done, you have to live with it – a tattoo won't wear off. That's why it's illegal to tattoo someone under the age of 18.

If you want a tattoo, only go to a licensed tattoo parlour as tattoos must be done under totally hygienic conditions. If the needles aren't sterile, there's a risk of infection such as tetanus or HIV.

Surveys show that 75% of people who have a tattoo eventually regret it and seek advice about how to get it removed. It is possible to remove tattoos by laser treatment, but it is very expensive. So think twice before you get a tattoo!

Temporary tattoos

Temporary henna tattoos are very fashionable, but they too can lead to health problems. Skin specialists say that the henna goes beneath the epidermis (top layer of skin) and can cause irritation.

Never have a black henna tattoo. This is because a chemical called PPD is sometimes added to pure henna to make black henna. PPD is black hair dye and should only be used in a very diluted form or there's a risk that it could leave an unsightly scar.

Discuss why you think tattoos are so popular. What reasons are there against having a permanent tattoo? What health risks are there from having a temporary tattoo?

FOR YOUR FILE

Write a story or a playscript about someone who gives in to pressure from their friends and has a tattoo, and then regrets having had it done.

Health care check – body piercing

Body piercing is increasingly popular. There's no age limit for getting pierced, but it must be done by someone who's been trained and who uses sterilised equipment. You should also weigh up the health risks, which include infections, bleeding and skin damage.

What do you think?

"I wanted to show my independence, so I got my ears and eyebrow pierced."

Max

"My mates all had piercings, so I got some. It's no big deal."

Jo

"I did it 'cause it's fashionable."

Paul

"I had it done for a dare to impress my boyfriend."

Min

❶ Why do you think body piercing has become so popular? What do you think are the main reasons why people get their bodies pierced?

❷ "Body piercing should be as strictly controlled as tattooing." Say why you agree or disagree with this view.

17 CHANGING RELATIONSHIPS

Friends and family

Aim: To explore your changing relationships with friends and family, and how to deal with these changes (PSHE 3e, 3f, 3h)

How to get a better deal

Do you feel that your parents give you less freedom than you're entitled to – much less than your friends, for example? Usually this is because they genuinely worry about you, about how you'll keep us with your schoolwork if you stay out too late and too often; about their fear (if you're a girl) that you may be attacked or raped if you travel home alone at night, or end up pregnant if you stay all night at a party; about their terror that you may have had an accident or be in trouble if you don't come home at a pre-arranged time. All these are to some extent realistic fears; they could happen. But these fears are relatively easy to deal with, so long as they're brought into the open and talked about.

It's more difficult if your freedom is restricted just because your parents have fixed ideas about what 'ought' or 'ought not' to be allowed at a particular age, or if strict rules are laid down which don't seem to make real sense to you. It's quite reasonable to tell your parents that you're the only one of your friends not allowed to do something special – but it has to be done really tactfully. It's easy to rub parents up the wrong way by pointing out how much more freedom your friends are given by their parents. 'But Tom's parents always let him ...' is likely to be met with only one response: 'Well, your parents don't.'

Points to remember

- They see themselves as good parents. Bring home the friends who are allowed extra freedom, so that your parents can see that they're not wild tearaways who will lead you into deep trouble.

- Aim for small concessions at first. i.e. negotiate an extra hour or two out when there's no school the next day.

- Once you've won that concession, try hard to keep your side of whatever bargain was struck. If you do stick to the agreed limits, it's more likely they'll agree to your next request.

- Try to get them to say exactly what is worrying them, rather than merely saying, 'You're too young!" There's nothing you can do suddenly to age yourself, but you may be able to reassure them about specific worries.

FROM E FENWICK AND T SMITH, *ADOLESCENCE, THE SURVIVAL GUIDE*

① **Summarise what this article says about how to get a better deal.**

② **Do you agree that understanding where your parents are coming from can help you get what you want?**

③ **Do you think putting this advice into effect will work? Or do you already take this advice?**

Choose a common parent-teenager situation and role play (a) how not to get what you want, and (b) how to get what you want, using one or two of these points of advice.

The trouble with friends

Fighting over a boy

If a girlfriend steals or snogs your boyfriend, then it's up to you whether you choose to forgive her. If you think the friendship is worth saving, then you'll need to have an honest chat with her about it. Ask her if she feels she needs to compete with you or assert her power over you. (That'll get her thinking.) You'll soon know if she's being honest and she realises what a huge mistake she's made.

What if you and a friend meet someone at the same time and you both really like him? Once again, talk about it. Friendships are not worth breaking up over a boy. True sisterhood is not about being competitive, but about supporting each other.

Speaking up

Let your closest friends know if you're upset by something they've said or done. It can be really difficult being honest with a close friend because

you have to strike a balance of not accusing them but getting your point heard. In any friendship it's important we tell each other when we're upset with one another. Anything we hold on to will only magnify itself and, however deep we think it's buried, it will inevitably rear its head later on.

If you do end up having a big row with a friend, then hopefully there will be a time when you decide to make up. It can be healthy to argue occasionally, because in a way you're saying that you know the friendship is strong enough to be able to have a fight and still be best mates at the end of it.

Letting go of friends

There are also so-called friends in our lives that aren't really good for us. Sometimes you have to accept that a friendship has changed and you no longer share the same interests. It's okay to know that you can move on from these friendships and create new ones.

The people you surround yourself with reflect how you feel about yourself. If you had more respect for yourself you would begin to move away from certain people because you realise that you deserve better friends than them.

FROM *SISTERS UNLIMITED* BY JESSICA HOWIE

 ❶ **Discuss what you have learned about friendships.**

❷ **Have you ever been in any of the situations Jessica Howie describes? How did you deal with it? Could you have dealt with it differently?**

FOR YOUR FILE

"My closest friend puts me down in front of boys" Samantha, 16.

Write a reply to Samantha.

 ❶ **"Men manage friends differently to women." Do you think this is true? List the differences between how a man and a woman would handle a difficult situation with a friend.**

❷ **Discuss what you think Jessica Howie means when she says, 'The people you surround yourself with reflect how you feel about yourself'?**

Exploring love

Aim: To explore what love is and how there are different kinds of love (PSHE 3b, 3e)

What is true love?

"Total trust and acceptance of someone." *Bill*

"Love means caring more about that person than you do about yourself."
Roshi

"There is no such thing as true love. It's an invention of the media."
Fabien

"True love is a unique chemistry between two people."
Mary

"True love? It just means wanting to spend all your time with another person, have fun and share things."
Josh

What love wasn't and what love is

Misha thinks about some of her early brushes with romance, and comes to see love in a completely new light...

I had the usual romanticised ideals of love. I could imagine nothing more fulfilling than being wanted and loved by a gorgeous boyfriend. I wished for the gaze of a boy – any boy – to fall on me. At first I went out with boys simply because I was so flattered to be asked.

I was thrilled the first time someone said they loved me, but then I would turn over in my head the various things that the words 'I love you' really mean. I wanted to be told that I was smart and funny, and beautiful; sometimes I was lucky and got to hear just that, although later I wondered if the boy really meant it, or if he was simply using the right words to get him 'further'.

Despite all these doubts and knowing the games I was playing with my image, like many of my friends I gave in to the pressure of having a boyfriend, any boyfriend. I thought I could find my identity

and my confidence in my boyfriend.

I relied on him far too much. In fact I doted on him so that I wouldn't be dropped; not because I was crazy about the boy but because I was dependent on the love he was supposed to represent. I thought that was love. All I was doing was setting myself up for self-pitying nights spent waiting for him to call, and missing my girlfriends and family as I gave all my spare time to one boy.

It took a long time for me to realise what was going on. That old saying that 'you are the only person who will never leave you' is so very true. We must learn to rely on ourselves, to trust ourselves, to respect and, most importantly, to love ourselves. It's one of the biggest lessons of our lives: to find true love, you must first love yourself.

When I had pride in myself first, people looked at me in a different light. Suddenly I was worth knowing, even though I was essentially the same person I'd always been. It's just that this time I believed it.

For a long time, love had one

definition for me: romance with a boy. Now I know that there are so many different kinds of love, and so many different motivations for loving. That the love of good friends and family are just as cool. That they might last a lot longer than the boy who's all over you today and bored with you tomorrow. Our need for love means that we seek it constantly and that we mistake possessiveness, lust, and giving up yourself for another, for love.

FROM *GIRLS' TALK* BY MARIA PALLOTTA-CHIAROLLI

❶ **What was wrong with the romantic idea of love that Misha had originally?**

❷ **What makes her new idea of love different from selfishness or big-headedness?**

❸ **Do you agree that 'to find true love, you first must love yourself'?**

Do you really want a girlfriend?

Peer pressure is not a good reason for starting a relationship with a member of the opposite sex. A boy who is going out with a girl just to impress his mates is not likely to make a very good boyfriend, because he's obviously going to be more concerned with what they think as opposed to what she feels.

It's nice to find the idea of female company attractive after years of boyishly denying their existence and trying to avoid them at all costs. But it is easy for boys to look on having a girlfriend purely as a status symbol or image-booster.

Relationships that just bring grief are all too common and are ultimately pretty pointless. Where's the sense in having a relationship purely for the sake of it? In fact it is far more pleasurable and beneficial to remain single, and to spend time getting to know and developing your own personality and interests than rushing into a relationship.

Teenage magazines and teenage fiction on television are often to blame for urging their readers into believing that love affairs and relationships with the opposite sex are the be-all and end-all of teenage life. They aren't. You don't have to date anyone when you are a teenager, and you will still grow up to be a perfectly normal, happy and healthy adult. And in fact the more time you spend on your own, discovering who you are, what are your likes, dislikes, aims and goals in life, when you are a teenager, the more likely you are to sail comfortably on to adulthood.

FROM NICK FISHER, *BOYS ABOUT BOYS*

① **How important is peer pressure in the search for a partner? What can you do about this pressure? Do girls suffer from a similar peer pressure?**

② **Do you agree that the media is also to blame for pushing teenagers into relationships they don't really want?**

③ **Nick Fisher says that the best reason for getting involved in a romance is a desire for a 'deeper quality of relationship'. Can you describe what would make a relationship deeper?**

Think about these different types of love:
- romantic love
- possessive love (obsession)
- sexual love (lust)
- platonic love (love for friends and relatives).

Write a short play or design a cartoon strip or a poster to show these different types of love.

18 COPING WITH CRISES

Separation and divorce

Aim: To explore the effects of family breakdown on young people (PSHE 3e, 3f, 3i, 3j)

Dealing with family breakdown

Research shows that around half of all divorces will occur within the first 10 years of marriage – often when children are still living at home. In fact, one in four children will experience their parents' divorce before they reach 16. What effect does separation and divorce have on children and families, and how do young people cope with these difficulties?

Surviving divorce

Divorce: It's a really hard thing to go through, says Jessica Howie...

I found my parents' divorce very painful and difficult. I was one of the last of my friends to have parents that split up and I thought I didn't have a right to be upset because everyone else had been through it before me.

Because I hid how I felt, I compensated by getting into drugs, booze and boys. When my parents separated I reached a new level of self-destructiveness. I was 14 at the time and just starting to come into my sexuality and have boyfriends. What I really needed was a safe place to show my feelings, and to have more communication with my parents about how I felt.

If your parents have split, it's okay for you to be upset about it. It is a very painful thing to go through and you're having to adapt to a completely different family unit. We all have different needs at times like this and it's important to say them to our parents. Often they're going through so much themselves that they don't realise you're finding it hard as well, and they might even lean on you for support.

How you can help yourself:

- Tell your parents how you're feeling; if you have a sibling, maybe confide in them, too.

- Your friends will rally round if you let them know you need them.

- Speak up and even get outside help if you need to.

- If you feel angry, allow yourself those. Don't try and protect your parents from your feelings – they are valid and important.

- Tell your parents that you don't want to feel like you're in the middle of their arguments.

Even if everyone you know has been through their parents splitting up, it doesn't devalue your pain and hurt. It is a really hard thing to go through.

FROM *SISTERS UNLIMITED* BY JESSICA HOWIE

 1 Discuss what you have learned about the effects of divorce.

2 Why did Jessica Howie behave in a self-destructive way when her parents were separating? How would you advise her to deal with it differently?

Deciding your future

When your parents split up, usually your parents will decide who it's better for you to live with. Don't feel guilty if you have a preference, though – it's your life. But if you don't want to say, just tell them to sort it out between themselves. In this case, they may have to go to court and let a judge make the decision. A court welfare officer may visit to try and find out which parent you'd be better living with.

Then a decision has to be made about how often you see your other parent. Again, it's best if this is sorted out by your parents (with help from you) but, unfortunately, it doesn't always work out like that.

What happens if...

... one of your parents tries to stop the other one from seeing you?

The one who's being prevented from seeing you has to go to court and ask for a 'contact order'. This says when and where they are allowed to visit and for how long. If the court thinks one of your parents has got good reasons for not wanting you to see the other one, they will send a supervisor to be at the meetings.

... you don't want to see one of your parents?

Your other parent will have to go to court and persuade the judge that a 'contact order' shouldn't be given. This isn't easy because usually the courts think that it's better for children if they're in touch with both parents. A court welfare officer and a child psychologist may meet you to find your reasons for not wanting to see that parent.

Maintenance

Both your natural parents have a responsibility to make sure you're cared for and to help pay for the things you need. Usually the parent who isn't living with you full-time has to pay 'maintenance' to the other parent.

FROM *TELL IT LIKE IT IS: THE VIRGIN YOUNG PERSON'S SURVIVAL GUIDE* BY K MASTERS

❶ **What decisions have to be made about what's best for the children when parents separate?**

❷ **List five pieces of advice you would give to someone whose parents are splitting up, giving reasons for your choices.**

"My parents have split up. I live with my mum, and that's fine but she's constantly telling me how terrible my dad is, which I hate. I'd like to see dad more, but I don't like to upset my mum. My dad has invited me to go to India with him. I'd love to do this, but how can I leave mum on her own?"

Amy, 15

Write a reply to Amy.

Bereavement

The effects of bereavement

It doesn't matter what age you are when someone important in your life dies or leaves you. It is difficult to sort out your feelings and it doesn't help when people say you should be feeling a particular way. The simple fact is that whatever you feel is how you feel at that time. It may be difficult for others to understand you, but it does help if you can learn to recognise these feelings for yourself even if you cannot explain them to other people.

Probably the strongest feeling you will have is sadness. It is important to let this out – this is what grieving is. But you may also have feelings that are less obvious...

NUMBNESS

Simply feeling nothing when you think you should be very upset is scary. Sometimes it's nature's way of letting us take things in slowly until we are ready to manage how we feel.

WORRY

You may worry about the future and who will be there to look after you. You may feel weird if you find yourself talking to the person who has died or thinking that you can see them – but even adults do this.

ANGER

You may feel angry for no particular reason.

It's hard not being able to blame someone when a person you love or rely on no longer there for you and so some people blame those around them, like doctors and nurses if the person who died was ill.

GUILT AND REGRET

When someone dies, for whatever reason, it is very normal to feel that you could have done more or that you should have behaved differently. It's also natural to think 'If only I'd...'.

Whatever your feelings are when someone dies, they're natural for you at that time. It can help to talk to someone you like and trust.

FROM WWW.CHILDBEREAVEMENT.ORG.UK

Coping with grief

It is OK to:
- cry and feel low and depressed. You've lost a great deal
- feel angry, embarrassed and not want to talk about your feelings
- 'live in the past' for a while. It can help you to keep alive the memory of the person you have lost, but try not to let life pass you by
- have fun and enjoy life, forgive yourself for the fights and arguments and nasty things you might have said to the person who died
- go on living.

But it is not OK to:
- use drugs or alcohol to dull your senses. This can only act as an escape and hide the pain, not helping to heal it, and can lead to other problems
- do things with your anger that can hurt other people because you are hurting inside
- experiment casually with sex, just to get close to someone
- hide your feelings to protect other people still alive.

If you find yourself getting into this sort of behaviour, it is important that you seek extra help.

FROM WWW.CHILDBEREAVEMENT.ORG.UK

Feeling suicidal

We can be unprepared for the intense feelings that can follow a death and for the way in which a once familiar world is turned upside down. Faced with this devastation, some people find themselves thinking that the world without the person who has died is now too scary, lonely, or too strange to carry on. They might wish that they too were dead.

This is a common reaction, and for most people the feeling fades over time. If, though, you find yourself thinking more and more about killing yourself, then it is really important that you find some support and help to get you through this difficult time.

WHO CAN YOU TALK TO?

● Talk to someone you know, like a friend, someone in your family, a teacher that you trust, your doctor.

● Ring a confidential helpline like ChildLine (0800 11 11), the Samaritans (08457 90 90 90) or Cruse Youth Helpline (0808 808 1677).

FROM WWW.RD4U.ORG.UK/PERSONAL/WHEN/SUICIDAL.HTML

① Discuss what you have learned about understanding your feelings when someone dies, and coping with grief.

② List five things that you can do to help cope with bereavement.

③ List five things that you can do to help a friend who has just been bereaved.

It happens to us all

We still have hang-ups about death. True, Britain's stiff upper lip may have quivered when Princess Diana died, but that was the exception that proved the rule. Often we're just uncomfortable tackling extreme emotions. But, on top of that, death is closely linked to religion and faith, which we tend to think of as private. When we do discuss it, we bring out all sorts of euphemisms – it's hardly surprising if young children get confused. "Grandma's passed away." "When's she coming back?"

Ironically, children in the 21st century are surrounded by death. But it's only make-believe, a screen fiction – playground games, video games, action movies. "In poor countries children have fewer problems with death," says Dr Colin Murray Parkes, a bereavement expert. "They see dead bodies, rotting corpses. Here people protect children from that kind of thing, assuming it must be traumatic. In fact, the opposite is true."

FROM THE ISSUE: BEREAVEMENT, *TES*

① Discuss whether you agree that children in different parts of the world have different attitudes to death.

② Why do you think death is such a taboo subject in our culture? What effect does people not talking about it have?

Research how different religions or cultures deal with death. Talk to members of different faiths. How do their mourning rituals help them to deal with death?

Write a reply to this email sent to a teenage online advice column.

"My lovely gran died suddenly of a heart attack three months ago. I feel so depressed I don't know what to do. I go round like a zombie most of the time, then I'm really snippy with my mum and my mates. I just feel like, why has she died and not me?"

Sara, 13

Leaving home

Aim: To explore the reasons why young people leave home, and what options are available to them (PSHE 3f, 3i)

Why go?

"Because family life is awful."

"To go to college or university."

"To travel abroad."

"Because my parents kicked me out."

"To live with my partner."

"To become more independent."

"To escape violence at home."

Discuss the reasons that young people may have for leaving home. Which are the three best reasons? Which are the three worst? Share your lists with other groups and justify your decisions.

Leaving home – Lisa's story

My name is Lisa. I am 19 years old. I'm not what you'd call a typical teenager who fought with their mum and dad all the time, but I had a very bad relationship with my mother. I was in and out of care from the age of 11. It was around my 16th birthday when she kicked me out. I felt like I was on my own in the big, bad world.

The first night I slept rough under a porta-cabin. This was going to get either easier or a lot harder. The next night was a godsend: I broke into a church, and it became my home, at least for the next few days.

After a few weeks of sleeping rough, I finally decided to do something, so I went to the Social Work Department. They got me into a hostel and I finally had a bath, clean clothes and a sense of warmth. I started to spend a lot of time with people my age, and started to learn that I wasn't alone.

In 2002 my mother died. That was when I found out that all the time we were arguing, it was my mum being unwell. So now I no longer blame myself for what happened between the both of us.

I am now living in supported accommodation, I have had a steady partner for nearly three years, and I have enrolled at college. It's when you're hardest hit that you must not quit.

FROM WWW.LEAVINGHOME.INFO

 Discuss what you have learned about how difficult life at home can be for some young people. How well do you think Lisa dealt with the situation? Would you have done anything differently?

Running away

When things go wrong at home, some people feel as if the only answer is to run away. Before you do this – talk to someone. Your parents are the best people to talk to because they can change things. Also, they may not be aware how you feel because you've been bottling it up. If you've got into trouble, they will have to know sooner or later, and will probably be more understanding than you think.

But if you can't talk to your parents, then talk to anyone you trust, such as a grandparent or a helpline. Running away may seem like an answer to your problems but usually it isn't. It's dangerous and difficult, and will almost certainly make those who love you sick with worry.

 What three pieces of advice would you give to someone who is thinking about running away?

A place of your own

If you decide to move out, what kind of accommodation is available?

Private rented accommodation

Houses, flats, bedsits or rooms rented out by landlords are the most common type of housing available to you when you leave home. Often you will have to share with others, and the standard of accommodation may vary. Renting can be done quite quickly and easily. However, rents can be high, and most landlords ask for a deposit and one month's rent in advance. They also are often wary of renting to young people on benefits.

Social rented housing

This refers to flats and houses rented out by local councils and housing associations. You may have to wait before you even get onto a waiting list, and single young people come lower down the priority housing list than families and couples. However, social housing tenants have better rights and usually pay lower rents than people in private rented accommodation.

Hostels

Hostels (not hotels!) are special types of accommodation catering for young people. Emergency hostels provide rooms for just a few nights. Women's refuges are for women who have escaped from a violent situation at home. Hostels vary a lot in their size and standard, and often have waiting lists. They may, however, suit your specific needs for a short time.

Buying a home

Get real. Either you've landed the job of a lifetime or you've got very generous parents. Buying a property is not a serious option for most young people!

Discuss the advantages and disadvantages of each type of accommodation. Then design an information leaflet aimed at young people looking for their first place away from home.

Leaving home and the law

The law says that young people under 18 are in 'the custody and care' of their parents. This means that, strictly speaking, they need their parents' permission to leave home. In fact, if a 16- or 17-year-old leaves home without their parents' permission, courts only order them to return if they are in danger or cannot look after themselves.

Under the Children Act (1989), 16- and 17-year-olds who are 'in need' should have accommodation provided to them by local authorities. However:

- suitable accommodation for young people is not always available
- income support is not available to all 16- and 17-year-olds.

You cannot buy or rent a house if you are under 18.

> **FOR YOUR FILE**
>
> **Write a short article for a teenage magazine entitled 'Thinking of leaving home?'.**

19 CHALLENGING OFFENSIVE BEHAVIOUR

Understanding prejudice

Aim: To understand what prejudice is, to explore where prejudice comes from, and how prejudice can lead to discrimination (Citizenship 1b, 2a, 2b, 2c/PSHE 3a, 3c)

What is prejudice?

Are you prejudiced? Most people think that they treat other people fairly. However, often we treat people according to opinions we have already formed about them. Here's an example:

Prejudice is when you have made up an opinion about somebody in advance. For example, being prejudiced about people who shave their heads would include thinking they are more likely to start fights, simply because of their appearance. The truth is a lot more complicated.

We often fit people into groups – black, white, male, female, young or old, and when we put people into groups, we can expect members of that group to behave in a particular way. This can lead to prejudice. For example, you may know lots of young people who enjoy loud music and going to parties. It doesn't mean that all young people are loud troublemakers.

 Imagine these roles – mother, father, brother and sister. List the prejudices you think would annoy each person. Discuss what you think the most common prejudices are and why.

Case study: Robert

Robert was on his way home when he saw a scruffily-dressed teenager rush out of a shop clutching a purse. Robert got out his mobile phone to call the police and ran after the teenager so that he could tell the police where he was. He was surprised when he saw the boy stop and start talking to an old lady. Imagine his embarrassment when he found out that the boy lived in the same block of flats as the old lady. She'd been into the shop and left her purse on the counter. He was running after her to give it back.

 ❶ **Why did Robert think the boy was a thief? Was it the circumstances or his appearance?**

❷ **Have you ever misjudged a person because of their appearance or behaviour? Has anyone ever misjudged you?**

❸ **Are some people more likely to be misjudged than others? Why?**

Part of a group or not?

We like to surround ourselves with people who are similar to ourselves because it is good to feel that you belong to a group. A group can be your family, people your age, your class at school, the members of a sports club or the members of a church. As humans, we immediately prefer those people in the same groups as ourselves; we have a natural tendency against people in different groups.

 ❶ **List all the groups you are in. Write down ways you think these groups behave.**

❷ **Compare your list with your partner's. Discuss whether these behaviours are fair. Or have you some prejudices about the groups you have listed?**

Looking at prejudice

Where does prejudice come from?

There are many different arguments suggesting where prejudice comes from.

We are born with it
It's natural for humans to compete. In the past this was for land and food, now it's exams, sporting events, or for jobs.

It's passed on to the next generation

Think about the games you were encouraged to play as a child. Were boys encouraged to play football and girls to play with dolls? Such behaviour reinforces prejudice about the opposite sex.

Going with the majority
People find it easier to go along with what other people are doing and copy other people's prejudices.

Scapegoating
This is when it's convenient to blame a problem on one group of people. For example, blaming unemployment on illegal immigrants when really there are problems in the economy.

Narrow minded or rigid views
Psychologically, some people have a greater likelihood of developing prejudices against new or unfamiliar groups, because they find it hard to accept new ideas and are more comfortable with familiar situations.

 Look at the causes of prejudice. Which do you think are the strongest factors in creating prejudice? Give reasons for your views.

Prejudice and discrimination

Prejudice may be wrong, but it's not against the law. We all have occasional thoughts about groups which may be incorrect. However, if these thoughts become commonplace and we choose to act on them, this then becomes discrimination.

Some forms of discrimination are against the law in the UK. These include the following:

- **Sexual discrimination**
- **Racial discrimination**
- **Age discrimination**
- **Religious discrimination**

 ❶ **Can you think of any other forms of discrimination?**

❷ **What do you think the most common kind of discrimination is in your local area? Give reasons for your views.**

 Design a poster against some form of discrimination. Compare your poster with other groups.

Fighting discrimination

Aim: To understand that there are laws and equal opportunities policies to combat discrimination, and to explore what you can do about discrimination (Citizenship 1b, 2a, 2b, 2c/PSHE 3a, 3c)

Discrimination and the law

There exists a wide range of laws outlawing many forms of discrimination, such as racial discrimination. There are several laws that the government uses against racist behaviour:

- **The Race Relations Act** (1976) and **Regulations** (2003) makes it illegal for anyone to discriminate on the grounds of race, colour, nationality, or ethnic and national origins.
- **The Crime and Disorder Act** (1998) makes racial crimes carry a heavier sentence.

Equal opportunities policies

On a local level, many employers and local organisations have equal opportunity policies to make sure no discrimination occurs. It may include practical examples of what is not acceptable, such as sexual harassment and sexist jokes against members of the opposite sex.

> "I think that discrimination against overweight people should be outlawed. It doesn't matter what I eat, I stay the same weight – yet people call me 'fatty'. I'm sick of being discriminated against."
>
> *Martha*

> "I hate the way everything is designed for right-handed people. How about a law to prevent discrimination against the one in 10 of us who are left-handed?"
>
> *Gemma*

 Do you think there should be laws to prevent discrimination against the people mentioned in the statements? Give reasons for your views.

Positive discrimination

Positive discrimination offers special opportunities for minority or disadvantaged groups. Supporters argue that this ensures that minority groups receive a fair access to things they would normally be excluded from. Critics of positive discrimination argue that it still produces discrimination, because it discriminates against those who would otherwise have access to those things.

Case study

In the UK in the mid-1990s, the Labour party decided it wanted more women in Parliament. In key constituencies that it was likely to win, the Labour party decided that only women could apply to become Labour candidates. This policy produced all-women shortlists and led to an increase in the number of women MPs. However, the practice was declared illegal by the courts – which argued that such positive discrimination was against the law.

> "All discrimination should be illegal."

> "Positive discrimination is necessary so that minority groups can be fairly represented in education and government."

 Look at these two statements. Which do you agree with? Give reasons for your views.

Taking a stand

The problem with discrimination is that many people don't know how to fight it when they encounter it. It takes courage. Here are six ideas for fighting discriminatory behaviour.

1 Don't ignore it, report it. If you witness discriminatory behaviour, report it to the police. Don't put yourself at risk of physical harm, but don't ignore the problem.

2 Complain – if you see discrimination on TV or hear it on the radio, contact the Advertising Standards Authority; if you read it in a newspaper or magazine, write to the editor of the publication; if you see it on a website, complain to the internet provider.

3 Don't tolerate friends who express discriminatory attitudes or behave in a discriminatory way.

4 Don't vote for political parties, such as racist political parties, who openly discriminate against minority groups.

5 Don't buy CDs or DVDs made by musicians who express prejudiced views.

6 Don't accept arguments that people use to justify prejudiced behaviour. Find out the real facts for yourself.

Challenging the myths about asylum seekers

Recent information released by the Race Equality Council in Dorset challenged the myths around asylum seekers.

Myth	Reality	
Most asylum seekers are just here looking for work.	Not true. An adult asylum seeker receives less than £40 a week, and is not permitted to work.	
Asylum seekers take all the taxpayer's money in the UK.	Not true. The UK gives asylum seekers less financial support that many other European countries, including Belguim, Ireland and Denmark.	
Britain is soft on asylum seekers.	Not true. In recent years, the countries hosting most asylum seekers were Germany, Pakistan and Iran. Out of a list of 36 countries that took in asylum seekers in 2001, the UK was 19th.	
More asylum seekers commit crime.	Not true. A recent report by the Association of Chief Police Officers confirmed that there is no evidence of a higher rate of crime among asylum seekers and refugees.	

 Look at the report. Was there any information that surprised you? Why? Do you think most people have an accurate image of asylum seekers?

20 REVIEWING AND RECORDING YOUR LEARNING

What you have learned

Aim: To review and record what you have learned from studying the units in *Your Life 4*

How to use this section

- Think about what you have learned in each of the four sections of the course.
- Use the questions below on each section to draft a statement about the knowledge and skills you have developed from studying the units in that section.
- In your statements include any important views, expressing your attitudes and values that you have formed as a result of considering and discussing particular topics.

> Here's what Jemma, 15, wrote as part of her statement about what she had learned from the unit on sex and contraception in the 'Keeping healthy' section.
>
> *I learned how important it is to think about sex in the context of a relationship and to discuss things fully with your partner before you have sex. It made me aware of the risks of having unsafe sex and the need to take precautions to protect yourself, not only from getting pregnant but from catching a sexually transmtted infection. Discussing the difficult decisions that you have to face if you get pregnant as a teenager made me realise that I don't believe abortion is right. It made me more determined than ever not to be pressurised into having sex till I feel I'm ready for it.*

Section 1: Developing as a citizen

Use these questions to help you to draft a statement about what you learned from this section.

What did you learn...

... about Britain as a diverse society? (Citizenship 1b, pages 6–9)
- about how the UK developed its diverse national identity, and about how Britain has benefited from ethnic diversity
- about what it means to be British.

... about human rights? (Citizenship 1a, pages 10–13)
- about the human rights that underpin society and the responsibilities we have to respect other people's rights.

... about rights and responsibilities? (Citizenship 1a, 1h, pages 14–19)
- about the rights and responsibilities of young people, workers and consumers
- about the legislation that defines responsibilities and protects these rights.

... about the law of the land? (Citizenship 1a, 1c, pages 20–23)
- about the different ways that laws are made
- about the criminal and civil justice systems.

... about crime and punishment? (Citizenship 1a, pages 24–29)
- about the age of criminal responsibility
- about ways of tackling antisocial behaviour and their effectiveness
- about youth crime and the process of youth justice
- about different types of punishment, their aim and their effectiveness.

... about your government? (Citizenship 1c, 1d, pages 30–35)
- about the structure and organisation of Parliament
- about how MPs are elected, and about the importance of voting.

... **about your council?** (Citizenship 1d, 1f, pages 36–41)

● about the structure and organisation of local government
● about what devolution is, and how local government is being changed to involve people more in decision-making.

... **about working for change?** Citizenship 1f, 3b, 3c, pages 42–45)

● about local and national pressure groups
● about how to set up a pressure group and how to mount a campaign in your local area.

Section 2: Understanding yourself

What have you learned from this section? Use these questions to help you to draft a statement.

What did you learn...

... **about developing your identity and image?** (PSHE 1a, 1b, 1c, 1d, pages 46–49)

● about what influences your behaviour
● about your identity and character, and the image you want to convey of yourself
● about what kind of adult you want to be.

... **about managing your emotions and moods?** (PSHE 1a, 1b, 1c, 1d, 3e, 3f, pages 50–53)

● about how to recognise and manage your feelings and moods, and how to deal with disappointment
● about how to behave assertively.

... **about planning your future?** (PSHE 1f, 1g, pages 54–59)

● about the career and educational opportunities open to you
● about what personal qualities you have and which career paths might be suitable for you
● about work experience.

... **about managing your money?** (PSHE 1e, pages 60–63)

● about budgeting, bank accounts and saving.

Section 3: Keeping healthy

Use these questions to help you to draft a statement about what you learned from this section.

What did you learn...

... **about healthy eating?** (PSHE 2g, pages 64–67)

● about attitudes to body shape, eating and dieting
● about how to develop healthy eating habits
● about obesity and junk food.

... **about safer sex and contraception?** (PSHE 2a, 2b, 2e, 2f, 3b, pages 68–71)

● about the risks involved in sexual activity, and what is meant by safer sex
● about different forms of contraception.

... **about drinking** (PSHE 2a, 2b, 2e, pages 72–73) **and smoking?** (PSHE 2a, 2b, 2e, pages 74–75)

● about the effects of drinking alcohol, and the risks of binge drinking and how to drink sensibly
● about how smoking and passive smoking can damage your health, and how to resist unhelpful pressure to smoke.

... **about health matters?** (PSHE 2a, 2e, 2g, pages 76–79)

● about what you need to know so that you can take responsibility for your own health
● about how to protect your hearing and to look after your skin
● about the dangers of sunbathing, tattooing and body piercing.

Section 4: Developing relationships

What you learned from this section? Use these questions to help you to draft a statement.

What did you learn...

... **about changing relationships?** (PSHE 3c, 3e, 3h, pages 80–83)

● about how to deal with conflict in your relationship with your parents, and how to deal with pressures on friendships
● about understanding the emotions you experience in close relationships, and what love is.

... **about coping with crisis?** (PSHE 3e, pages 84–89)

● about the impact of separation, divorce and bereavement on families and how to adapt to changing circumstances, such as leaving home.

... **about challenging offensive behaviour?** (PSHE 3a, 3c/Citizenship 1b, pages 90–93)

● about prejudice, racism and religious discrimination, and how to challenge offensive behaviour.

INDEX